# THE ECONOMICS OF LIFE

## A GUIDE TO PERSONAL ECONOMICS AND HAPPINESS

D. C. ANJARIA

Published by

D. C. ANJARIA

book@dcanjaria.com

# DEDICATED TO

All practitioners of the Economics of Life
who inspired this book –

Including Bill Gates and Azim Premji,
who I do not even know

Sam Pitroda
who I do know

Haresh Dholakia and Nalin Dholakia,
who through their practice inspired me

Principal S. V. Desai and his professors' team,
including Prof. D. D. Trivedi

Karnika, Wife, Guide, always on the path of what
matters in life, regardless of money

Dharit, Son, Pseudo-Publisher and Guide

Padmini, Daughter-in-law, Supporter and Guide to
the pseudo-publisher and the author

Armin, Grandson, Enforcer of the Balance of Life

There are many guides available to us that seek to help us achieve physical wellbeing and good health. However, there are few, if any, self-help guides for us to achieve economic wellbeing. The many guides that address our economic wellbeing mostly cover the field of where to invest money; but we need to know how to earn the money to invest and what to save and create our wealth and how to use it.

In fact, we are and remain prisoners in money-driven economies. Our key decisions to lead a happy life are dictated by money the jailer. Professional economists guide the governments to pursue policies to make us economically happy. But the only advice is to keep earning money and creating monetary wealth.

In fact, we are not always happy in these economic prisons. Here is a guide to happiness with money. And a guide to happiness without money!

Fortunately, we also inhabit an economy that is not driven by money alone. We have, can and must use our nonmonetary resources. We create our own economy. And we draw up our own economic wellbeing plan; we create our personal economics, nonmonetary resource based as well as money based.

You and I, non-economists, we are the masters of the science of economics. We dictate the science of economics by our personal economics.

Let us see how to break away from the prison: money-only economics.

Welcome to our own economics of our own life.

The Economics of Life.

# TABLE OF CONTENTS

# Chapter One

# Reader's Guide to This Book
## And a Lifelong Guide to Happy Economics

A Guide for You and Me – The Non-Economists

Our Life, Our Philosophy, Our Happiness, and Our Own Economics

The Goal of the Science of Economics

The Goal of Our Personal Economics

The Aim of a Broader Philosophy of Life

# A Guide for You and Me – The Non-Economists

This book is written for those of us ordinary human beings who value life and its qualities and who want to know how best to live in a society organized around money. Our guide for all economic circumstances – post-war, post-pandemic, post-financial crisis, and day-to-day life.

The book is not a business book meant for those professional economists who want to derive economic laws and rules from human behavior.

The book is based on the fundamental belief that economics is nothing if it does not concern us human beings, that economics is not a purely scientific discipline, where economic laws are derived by professional economists. Economic decision-making is also a personal discipline where most economic laws are and will be made by human beings for themselves, applied and practiced by them; all economic laws are not made for them, barring a few of the laws.

Professional economists need to understand the personal economic laws and economic decision-making process of the non-economists – us. We make the economics as much as we are governed by the scientific economics. The book is therefore a guide for us non-economists and an appeal to professional economists to take heed of us as economic agents.

# Our Life, Our Philosophy, Our Happiness, and Our Own Economics

What do we gain from this book?

This book does not seek to give you a philosophy of life to deal with the goal of achieving happiness by all means – monetary and non-monetary.

You have your own philosophy of life; the book seeks to give you an understanding of essential economics – both the science of economics and the economics of life, such that it would help you implement your philosophy of life and move closer to your goal of achieving happiness in life.

# The Goal of the Science of Economics

The currently practiced science of economics deals with the goal of achieving happiness only by means of money, believing that happiness can only be achieved by money, and more money. This book will guide you to happiness with money, more money, less money, and even no money.

The widely accepted aim of economics is to help you earn more money, under the assumption that the greater the money you will have, the happier you will be. The aim of economics of life has got to be to help you earn more happiness by means of money.

# The Goal of Our Personal Economics

The science of economics deals with the goal of achieving happiness by means of money in a society organized around money. Of course, you can achieve happiness through other means. But economic means of money are also essential to achieve happiness. Let us look at money and other means to derive happiness in life.

The economics of life are what life is all about, it is all about us, all about the economics that we believe in and pursue. We are not concerned with the science of economics and its rules; we are concerned about our own personal economics and rules we set for ourselves. The goal is the same as the science of economics, achieving happiness in life but by means that are both monetary and nonmonetary. Ignoring the money-only economics of the economists yet learning from their economics as seen by us.

# The Aim of a Broader Philosophy of Life

You govern and lead your life with your own philosophy implicit or explicit, about how to live happily. The aim of a broader philosophy of life as advocated in this guide will be to help you define what you should earn, and how to earn happiness or any other thing by monetary and non-monetary means. It is your own philosophy of life that defines and drives your personal economics as well as the science of economics. Thus, Economics of Life encompass all three drivers – personal philosophy, personal economics, and the science of economics.

# Chapter Two

# UNDERSTANDING OUR ECONOMIC PRISON

WE THE PRISONERS

WE NEED THE JAILER!

ECONOMIC PRISON POLICY MAKERS

NO ESCAPE FROM THE ECONOMIC PRISON

MONEY IS ESSENTIAL TO LIFE

WE ACCEPTED THE PRISON SENTENCE

PRISONERS CAN BE HAPPY, TOO

ECONOMICS AT OUR SERVICE, OUR LIFE

WE, NOT MONEY, TO DICTATE OUR LIVES

HAPPY LIFE WITH UNDERSTANDING OF ECONOMICS AND SETTING PERSONAL RULES

KNOW THE ESSENTIAL ECONOMICS – RIGHT HERE!

Let us start on the road to understanding the life we spend in the "economy," the science of economics, our personal economics, and the economics of life.

# We the Prisoners

We are all prisoners of money.

Condemned to live in our prison known as the economy.

Money is our jailer.

# WE NEED THE JAILER!

We cannot do anything without the jailer permitting.

We cannot escape from the prison; the economy is everywhere.

Just to be able to live, we need our jailer, and the jailer's permission to do what we want to do.

We need to learn to live in the economy, within the bounds set by money, not let money hold us prisoner against the larger happiness we seek.

We need to learn the economics of life in prison.

# ECONOMIC PRISON POLICY MAKERS

But the jailer is not entirely free to set the rules of our lives.

The prison policy is set by the economists and politicians who run the economy, who set the rules that govern our daily lives. The jailer must obey the policy while setting the rules that govern our prison stay – our lifetime.

# No Escape from the Economic Prison

There are those who seek to escape the prison and live outside the economy. They believe they can escape the money-driven economy altogether. In fact, those who seek to live outside the money-driven economy are still dependent on money. They may not talk to money directly. But they have to depend on other prisoners to help them live without direct contact with money. If the saints and priests truly retire from all economic decision making, they can, but their followers and the faithful still need to support them the retirees with monetary resources.

Whether we escape to deep Amazon jungles or African bush or the highest snow-covered mountain peaks of the Himalayas or alpine white slopes, the economy is there everywhere. Escape sanctuaries are all part of the economy.

By retiring to the bushes, mountains, or jungles, the saints who think they have escaped the prison are the ostriches who do not see the jailer – money. It is money that still governs their lives under the care of their fellow prisoners, be it the followers of the saints or the family members or even the donors and governments who "take care of them." Notice that even the Vatican has a Bank! Most religious brotherhoods live on alms. Whether the Christian monks with a vow of "poverty" or the Hindu saints living on the heights of the Himalayas, they may personally live away from money-based civilization, but they cannot escape money or the material world.

We can set our own rules within some limits permitted by the jailer – money and not be driven entirely by money; even when you escape the material world, you need money; we can form small groups where we help one another. We can even be part of a large community, but in the end, we have to interact with the jailer. We may not wish to be obsessed with money, but we need money to be able to live.

# Money is Essential to Life

It is precisely to enable us to live, as part of a community, that the economy was created and money was invented and called in as our help, to enable us to live and function as part of the society we co-habit with others.

No matter how much ascetic seclusion our saints may practice, no matter how high up the Himalayas they go, they remain part of the human community, part of the economy, with money needed to live. Where the money comes from may differ, but neither the saints nor the lay followers like us, can do without money. At one point or another, directly or indirectly, each of us needs money.

# WE ACCEPTED THE PRISON SENTENCE

The economy was not intended to be a prison; we have had to accept voluntarily the economy as our collective home. It became our prison because we cannot live except as part of the economy. We need to exchange goods and services with our other fellow community members. The exchange is now nearly impossible except with a common measure of exchange – money.

Just as the economy was not intended to be a prison, money was not intended to be its jailer.

All economies run on money as the vehicle. As members of the economy, we need to ride money as our vehicle to our chosen destinations, to satisfy our needs. Money keeps us as part of the economy, and we cannot live except as part of the economy.

# PRISONERS CAN BE HAPPY, TOO

As we will always remain in our economic prison with money as its jailer, we have no option but to accept the rules of the prison and obey them, and no option but to accept the rules set by our jailer.

Fortunately, the good news is that we can live happily ever after if we accept the prison rules and cooperate with the jailer. Making friends with our jailer – money, is our best chance to enjoy our prison – the money-driven economy. In this economy, we can get easily marginalized without enough money, so let us be happy with money.

In other words, a happy life is possible for us still as prisoners. The prison was in fact created to make us happy. The jailer was called in to guide us to a happy life.

So let us learn the prison rules and the jailer's instructions on how to live happily.

Let us learn the economics of life in the prison.

Economic rules with money as the vehicle set the economics of life. Let us understand the economics of life to lead ourselves to a happy life, within the prison, with no need to dig up a channel to escape to some happy life outside the economy and without money.

# ECONOMICS AT OUR SERVICE, OUR LIFE

What matters is our lives, our life, not economics.

Economics matters in our lives because we cannot escape from our prison – the economy. Economics matters because we cannot do without the guiding force of the economy – money.

Yet, both the money and the economy as a whole must serve our life for us to be happy, for us to guide our lives to our chosen destinations of happiness.

Let us not reverse the roles. We cannot make our lives subservient to economics. We cannot let the prison and the jailer dictate our lives, our free lives.

# WE, NOT MONEY, TO DICTATE OUR LIVES

If we do not understand the prison policy and the jailer's instructions, they will dictate our lives. If we understand the rules of the economy, the use of money, we can make our lives happy, even inside the prison.

If we let money dictate our lifestyles, money will become the master of our lives. Let us not spend our lives trying to acquire money. Acquiring money cannot be the purpose of our life. We must define the purpose of our life and make money serve our purpose.

Yes, our jailer can accept our own rules of our own economics, our personal economics, our economics of life, designed by us to be happy.

Yet the prison – the economy will have its own rules and the jailer its own instructions. But within the bounds of the economy, we can set our own rules of life. The question is – how do we set our own rules to be happy? The answers follow.

# HAPPY LIFE WITH UNDERSTANDING OF ECONOMICS AND SETTING PERSONAL RULES

Understanding economics is the first step to traverse "two paths" to design our own economics of life.

The first path is for us to understand how the economy works, what money does – that is the world we live in. To be happy, even while remaining part of the economy, we can and must design our own rules of life.

But then there is another path that we need to traverse as well. That is a personally found path, which would go beyond the economy and money and focus on our rules of life. Having learnt the rules and the role of the economy and money, we need to bend them to serve our lives – the purpose of our life and the path we seek to a happy life. This new set of economic rules we determine will define our personal economics. Our own economics of life, our second path to a happy life.

# Know Essential Economics – Right Here!

What is essential for us to know about economics? Not knowing the essentials of economics can lead to unpleasant surprises in our life, lead us to a lot of unhappiness. For example, we cannot ignore the economics of inflation; inflation eats up our money stock, our savings. We must provide for inflation in making our rules of life. We cannot sustain our economic lives and achieve our lifelong goals if we have ignored the economics of inflation.

To learn about economics, we need not acquire a doctorate in economics. Need not turn ourselves into economists. There are professional economists who pursue economic studies. We need to learn from them the essential economics – the barest minimum to be able to guide ourselves through the vast prison we inhabit.

We start with understanding the Science of Economics.

# Chapter Three

# UNDERSTANDING OUR SCIENCE OF ECONOMICS

### SCIENTIFIC ECONOMISTS AND US

### WE MAKE ECONOMIC SCIENTISTS GO WRONG!

### WE MAKE ECONOMICS, NOT THE ECONOMISTS!

### ECONOMISTS TO MARRY OUR MICROECONOMICS WITH THEIR MACROECONOMICS – TO BE OUR GUIDES

There are two routes of our journey to happiness, via Two Economics – Scientific and Personal.

Here Is How the Science of Economics Works.

# SCIENTIFIC ECONOMISTS AND US

Traditional, professional economists like to think of economics as a science that can explain economic events by certain scientific rules that they think guide our behavior as economic agents, while taking diverse economic decisions. They treat the whole economy as a single entity. They derive macroeconomic rules and seek to explain what has happened and will happen – at the macro level, in the world of money.

At the ground level as well, professional economists treat us as economic agents, people who take economic decisions. They make assumptions about how we take economic decisions. The science of economics has even developed two special branches – Behavioral Economics and Experimental Economics. Through one, they seek to understand how we take decisions, and through the other, they check out various hypotheses by experimenting on us. For example, professional economists assume that all of us are rational human beings and seek to derive maximum benefit, using minimum resources. They assume we will always want to be wealthy and wealthier. They cannot understand those of us who seek to escape from the money-driven economies and do not seek wealth altogether.

Experimental economists set up test groups – individuals or communities and put them through some specific circumstances to see if we do indeed decide "rationally" – and always take economic decisions to increase our monetary wealth all the time.

With such hypotheses and assumptions, they conduct experiments on us to see whether the hypotheses are confirmed; just as the pure scientists also go by deriving rules by testing out their hypotheses. They study our behavior. They think they can fit our behavior into neatly derived scientific rules and understand how the macroeconomy moves. They also seek to understand our own personal economics, our micro-economics. And they think they can tell us what to do to achieve happiness and how to guide our lives to make the right economic decisions and be happy.

From the viewpoint of the economics of life, we can hope that the Experimental Economists will understand our decision making better, understand the role money plays in our lives, and the decisions we take around money and without money. Then, they would not just treat us as economic agents in the money-driven economy; they will examine our behavior in the non-monetary economy as well, and decisions we take as consumers, savers, investors, donors and as members of a specific community. This is already a move towards understanding our personal economics not just in money-driven economies but in communities organized around non-monetary economies as well. No wonder, given the importance of the Experimental Economics, the much-coveted Nobel Prize for Economics for 2021 was awarded by the Swedish Royal Academy to two experimental economists – Abhijit Banerjee and Esther Duflo of M.I.T.

# WE MAKE ECONOMIC SCIENTISTS GO WRONG!

Unfortunately, the economists often go wrong. They cannot always forecast macroeconomic events like price inflation or downward economic cycles. If economists could forecast major events with full clarity, there would be no volatility on Wall Street! Nor can economists always derive rules of our personal economics. That makes professional economists poor guides for us.

If professional economists often go wrong in predicting economic events that have an impact on our lives, the reason is that economics is not a science like physics, with clear rules that the economists think exist, but do not exist. We are creative human beings, rational or otherwise; our economic decisions and actions cannot be predicted by traditional economics. We pursue our happiness goal in our own way, some this way and some that way, and not as a group or a rational community. We may not accept the highest paying job, and be happy in pursuing our preferred activity – despite it being low-paying? We sympathize with the scientific economists who have to deal with us unpredictable beings, and yet be in a position to predict the resulting economic events at the macro level or micro level.

# WE MAKE ECONOMICS, NOT THE ECONOMISTS!

Economics and money did not drop from heavens like the entities that physicists study. Economics is a human science. Money is our human invention. The economy and the money move by decisions we make about our lives. We, the ordinary economic agents, not the professional economists, who guide the economic developments, who write the rules, who create a science of our own. This is our own "unscientific" personal economics.

It is we the ordinary economic agents who make economics. Economics is based on the collective economic decisions that we take, that create or make the macroeconomy. It is the personal economics we pursue that creates the microeconomy. When we buy things or services, when we sell them, when we build wealth in money and when we use our nonmonetary resources – these are all economic decisions. Through these personal economic decisions, through our view of money, we become the economy makers.

We reside in a money-driven broader economy, we do react to the scientific economics dictated by the economists and regulators, but we also pursue our own, personal economics without reference to money and monetary economic conditions and rules. We inhabit two worlds simultaneously – the official economy and the personal economy. We create both macroeconomics and microeconomics.

The fact is that economists often go wrong in forecasting even macroeconomic events, such as inflation or cost of living, or the real value of money, let alone our personal economic events, because they do not understand the rules that guide our personal economics.

Macroeconomics goes wrong if economists ignore microeconomics - the vast number of decisions made by us with our own personal economics. It is this vast number of decisions that all of us make as individuals that result in macroeconomic reality. It is this vast number of personal economic decisions that we take, often canceling one another's decisions, which create microeconomic reality. It is these vast number of microeconomic decisions that are clearly difficult to predict. The rules of our personal economics are not physical world laws. We make our rules, and we unmake them, albeit within the bounds of the economy and money – our jailer. The prison and the jailer make their rules for us, but, parallelly, can also set our rules consistent with our personal economics. We are not just scientific entities that follow predictable rules. We are creative beings who take economic decisions based on our own philosophy, our own feelings, our own rationale, all of these escape the scientific search of professional economists.

The professional economists do not touch our economic decisions if they cannot measure our decisions in terms of money. Here is another reason why they go wrong. We take many decisions effectively outside of the economic prison driven by money, and driven by our other motivations, using our other resources than money. When we fall in love with someone, do we think of money? When we give up our job because we do not "like" it, do we think of money? When we buy and consume expensive products and services, are we being rational and trying to maximize our savings or wealth? When we give away a larger share of our wealth, are we being rational about money? Economists just stop at our money-driven decisions and ignore our apparently irrational economic decisions.

# ECONOMISTS TO MARRY OUR MICROECONOMICS WITH THEIR MACROECONOMICS – TO BE OUR GUIDES

Unless professional economists relate their macroeconomics to the microeconomics that we pursue with our personal economics, they will often go wrong as they do. The science of economics has to adjust itself to the personal economics pursued by us as individuals or as communities. Economic researchers and academicians have to study how microeconomics impact their macroeconomics. Economic advisors have to take account of the personal economics framework to see how the economies they govern may be altered at our personal levels. The governments that follow economic advisors, as also the academic economist community - students, researchers and institutions of learning, the Economics faculty of universities, all of them have to pursue the microeconomics and relate it to their scientific macroeconomics, the objective being to reduce the incidence of error and distance between macro and micro economic worlds. Our creative, unscientific, irrational views have to be taken account of while trying to predict economic events.

Until economists advance this branch of study of microeconomics, their economic advice will not always be dependable by us. So do not depend on professional economists to let you guide your lives to happiness.

Goodbye, honorable economists!

# Chapter Four

# Understanding Our Economics of Life

The Science of Economics – What Is Right

The Science of Economics – What Is Wrong

Economists' Rational Hypothesis and Assumption

Getting the Science of Economics Right

The Macroeconomic Science - Cost Versus Benefits

We Still Need Macroeconomics

Learning From the Science of Economics - Setting Our Own Personal Economic Rules

Basic Economic Framework – Adapt to our Personal Economics

What Resources Do We Have?

Employ All Resources – Money Alone not to Dominate

Measure Nonmonetary Benefits as well as Monetary Benefits

The Personal Economics Framework

Personal Economics with Money

# The Science of Economics – What Is Right

Our journey to happiness in life goes via two economics – scientific and personal; we need to traverse both paths; we now know how the Science of Economics works; now, we focus on how the Science of Economics impacts our own Economics of Life.

Let us briefly try to understand how professional economists look at their "science" of economics. The science that the professional economists pursue deals with the basic question of how to perfect the use of limited resources to produce the maximum utility for all of us. If all of us, the world, all economies had at their disposal "unlimited" resources, the science of economics would not be needed! Economists from Adam Smith onwards use the term "utility" to define what is expected to be achieved, the output, the result. Utility is a material concept. Utility is defined in terms of money. If resources are limited in availability, then we would like to produce the maximum possible "utility" by consuming the minimum possible resources. The aim and the endeavor are seen as "scientific" and rational; material utility – why would you not maximize the money, the wealth?

The aim of economists is to help governments manage economies and economic systems. This is macroeconomics. This scientific approach to economics is pursued by professional economists at the macro level, where macroeconomics is studied, macroeconomic events are forecasted, and economic systems are managed. Within certain limits and exceptions, it works.

At the level of goods and services providers, economics is recognized as the social science that deals with the production, distribution and consumption of goods and services. This is microeconomics. Microeconomics is studied in the context where goods/services producers are expected to seek positive output from a given level of inputs.

So far so good; the scientific approach works at macro and micro levels.

Unfortunately, economics is still a social science and not a physical science, so economists often go wrong in forecasting macroeconomic events and successfully managing economic systems, if they ignore or do not understand the personal economics pursued by us at our individual level. Our personal economics also have an impact on macroeconomics; this is broadly not studied by the "scientific" economists. We will see how, later.

In summary, professional economic scientists may go wrong in understanding our personal economics. But their science of economics is not all wrong and is applicable at the macro and micro levels.

## WHAT IS RIGHT AT THE PERSONAL ECONOMICS LEVEL

Despite the difficulties of correct forecasting of economic events, the professional economists' approach is not all wrong; it is right at the base, and at the aim. Economics is pursued all for our happiness and good. Economists seek to educate us in the approach – to minimize resource consumption for maximum production, maximum happiness. Even if we as individuals do not figure in the science of economics as "active" agents who take part in this effort to use resources to produce our happiness, we must do that. Use as small a resource basket as possible and still be happy, because the earth has only limited resources and we humans are already using far more resources than available from our finite resource base of land, air, and water. We the non-economists must thank the professional economists for having brought the fundamental economic science to us and made us aware of the problem of limited resources we have at our disposal and the action needed to optimize the consumption of these limited resources to produce maximum possible happiness.

In fact, we, even as ordinary non-economists, know how to minimize our resource consumption and maximize our satisfaction and happiness. We practice economic understanding in our daily lives. How do we do this economic activity?

We do not spend all the money we earn; we save it for the future, and we invest it, and use the savings to maintain our lifestyles over time. We conserve our own personal, non-monetary resources – our time, our skills; we use them as members of society, often ignoring the monetary economics.

Farmers seek to produce the maximum possible harvest with minimum consumption of fertilizers or water, or even land. Companies seek to produce the maximum possible goods with minimum human resources or minimum inputs of raw materials or power or water. Our women are the most adept in the art and science of making us happy with the minimum foodstuff yet giving us good meals – not expensive!

Think of your profession or activity or lifestyle and you will know how you practice economics without understanding it scientifically.

So far, the scientific approach of economists works for us as well. Where it goes wrong is when macroeconomists do not factor in our will that governs our role as economic agents. That is the reason they often go wrong, as they work only with macro trends, not micro movement aggregates stemming from our role as decisionmakers, often overturning the professional economists' scientific interpretations.

Even when economists keep us in mind and study our decision making and our behavior, they go wrong in making assumptions about how we decide and behave. Behavioral Economics is an example of how economists seek to understand our decision-making process – scientifically, to understand the science of decision-making, not the motivations and preferences of our decisions. Take even the Experimental Economists; they too follow the scientific path of developing hypotheses of how we take economic decisions, and then test these hypotheses by experimenting on us. None of these two branches of economics study how these micro-decisions impact the macro-decisions.

There is still no link between macro and microeconomics. That is why we pursue our own economics, while they pursue their own macro-economics. The science of economics is still a poor guide for our economic pursuits, our lives, our path to happiness. That is why this book! Let us see how we pursue our own economics.

# ECONOMISTS' RATIONAL HYPOTHESIS AND ASSUMPTION

Traditional economists assume we are all rational human beings, who will always take rational economic decisions; the word "rational" being defined as decisions that would mean we would want to spend the least amount of "money" while desiring the maximum "utility" in terms of money. For example, we would like to spend the least possible amount for the best possible product we need to buy. We would settle for the highest possible salary or wages for the job or work we seek; we would quit the job if we got higher compensation for the same job if offered. We would prefer the highest possible return – interest or dividend – when we invest our savings. If we were offered a free gift, we would take it! We would in short want to build the highest possible monetary wealth. And all our decisions will be measured and driven by money, as "rational" human beings. We would not be "irrational" enough to refuse a higher paying job or better priced product or lower return on investments – in terms of money.

What this assumption of "rational" means in practice is that we would not want to be part of an economy that is outside of the money-driven economy, and search for rewards other than money, or giveaway our money, our services and time to others and be happy about the act. In other words, economists simply assume the "irrational" world does not exist – at least can be ignored.

It is precisely the basic assumption that the professional economists make that is problematic. They assume that each of us is a rational animal, and that we want to maximize what they term as utility or what we term as happiness. In reality, we take many decisions that are not rational – we do not always want to maximize our economic benefit. We take different decisions from the ones that are simply designed to maximize monetary economic benefits. So, we may not quit our job for more money elsewhere, because we like and are happy in our current occupation. If we like a product, we will buy it even if its pricing is premium. We would not want to risk our savings just for a higher return on some other investment which we may see as too risky for us. In fact, we may even consciously invest in assets of businesses that are "ethical" – so we will not buy products made by child labor, for example.

Lately, economists have realized the folly of this rational hypothesis. We now have behavioral economics and economists who have started looking at the rules by which we behave; in other words, take decisions. Unfortunately, even behavioral economists like to think of themselves as being in pursuit of the science of economics, science of economic decision-making by us, which they also assume would be "rational." They cannot think of us as irrational beings, behaving differently from the rational norms. Rational norms are all those decisions we have listed, all economic decisions that follow the goal of building monetary wealth by getting the highest possible reward from our activity, by spending the least possible money. Yet, the economists stick to their assumption of rationality, even as "assumed rational behavior" is not always what happens in our personal endeavor and is ignored by the economists.

# GETTING THE SCIENCE OF ECONOMICS RIGHT

Professional economists pursue their science and research by focusing on macroeconomy – events like inflation and productivity and financial stability. They seek their position as policy makers, as guides to governments and business regulators. They cannot guide us at individual level, only at the macro level.

If economists have to succeed in their social science, they ought to be effective "guides" to individual decision makers, to us as non-economists. It is only by economists' factoring in our decision-making results that the economists can serve their useful role as our guides – by marrying macroeconomics with our microeconomics. It is only by "synchronizing" the search for maximum utility or monetary prosperity at the global economy level with the same search by us at personal level, that economists will be able to guide us to derive sufficient satisfaction and happiness both at global economy level and individual personal level.

But let us not worry about the professional economists. They can guide us in a limited sense. We need to guide ourselves at the much larger individual level. We can still pursue the search for optimum resource consumption and produce maximum satisfaction, but while following our own personal economics. It is by following our personal economics that we can set our rules on how we will behave even while being imprisoned in the economy and instructed by money. We set our personal rules that will mesh with the prison policy and the jailer's instructions. Jailer's rules are set for money-driven economic prison. As long as we follow those rules, do not be surprised if the jailer accepts our non-money-based rules, as long as we do not harm our fellow prisoners, as long as we do not dig an escape channel out of the economic prison.

So let us accept to remain in the prison yet set the rules of personal economics we wish to see.

# THE MACROECONOMIC SCIENCE – COST VERSUS BENEFITS

Professional economists often but not always make mistakes in dealing with economic events and deciding what is right and what is wrong. They are right about resource consumption versus benefits we seek to derive. The science of economics, simplified for us, is essentially a cost-benefit analysis. Economists would like to believe and assume that we as rational human beings would want to derive the maximum benefits at the lowest costs. This also is not a wrong assumption, as far as it goes.

While the approach, the cost-benefit framework is valid, professional economists go wrong now with their approach applied to the fundamental economic measurement only in terms of money. So here comes money – not just as a facilitator and common exchange measure, but as the basis of all economics.

That is why all cost-benefit exercises are done in terms of money. Money is the primary and only measure of economic analysis. Along with rational hypothesis assumption, the use of money as the only measure of cost/benefit studies gets the professional economists in trouble in dealing with us. We the creative economic decisionmakers, we who take many decisions "irrationally" and not in terms of money. Even behavioral economists resort to understanding our behavior in rational and money terms, study how we take our economic decisions. But they cannot predict our behavior always correctly, and certainly not predict macroeconomic consequences of our own decisions, since we, the non-economists, as our own masters, do not always follow cost benefit exercises, not always thinking of money as our driver. Unable to forecast our behavior at the micro level, the economists also get it wrong at the macro level and are unable to forecast macroeconomic events if driven by non-money-oriented personal economics.

# WE STILL NEED MACROECONOMICS

We live in an economy and economy is understood by economists at the macrolevel. Many of their concerns at the macroeconomic level will be relevant concerns for us as well because they have an impact on our lives and livelihoods and on our personal happiness.

Macroeconomic concepts like price inflation directly impact our purchasing power, our savings, and investments values. Economists track at the full economy level measures such as consumption, savings, investments or returns on investments, and future value of money. Their conclusions at the economy level will have some relevance to our own personal economics. And other measures. We will review these macroeconomic measures much later in this book, after understanding the simplest economic model of macroeconomics.

Professional economists' model simplified to its core, concerns costs versus benefits. They seek "value added" by ensuring we obtain maximum monetary return vis-à-vis the costs incurred by us or resources consumed by us. What they seek at the economy level, we must also seek at our personal level. That is why we need help from macroeconomics that is relevant to our lives and our happiness.

# Learning From the Science of Economics - Setting Our Own Personal Economic Rules

We need to begin by first learning the economic framework. The simple economics of cost-benefit analysis is a framework we can certainly adopt and not worry about complex economic concepts.

We will certainly also try to understand the essential macroeconomic concepts that have a bearing on our lives, lives in the economic prison. But we will not remain confined to our prison cells; we will also set our own rules – by walking out in the fresh air where no money is needed, where we are allowed by the jailer to roam under the skies above the prison. We are obliged to follow the economic rules around "money"; but we also guide our lives with rules around "non-money" measures.

So, we will develop and adopt our own economics, our own rules.

# Basic Economic Framework – Adapt to our Personal Economics

We can adapt the professional economists' cost-benefit evaluation approach to our personal economics.

But we will not measure our costs and benefits in only monetary terms. We can and will count our costs in terms that are non-monetary as well, in terms of any resource that we need to employ to get the desired outcome for a happier life. We have many resources at our command, and we will employ the most productive resources to pursue our goals, to pursue happiness for us.

We will also measure the benefits the same way – not just in monetary terms but in non-monetary terms as well. We have many benefits we may look for while employing our available resources.

So, we accept the professional economists' simplified framework of monetary costs and benefits and look for a net gain. But we will not restrict this framework to money alone as the measure of our economic lives. We will determine our costs and benefits in any terms for the resources we employ and for the benefits we expect.

# WHAT RESOURCES DO WE HAVE?

Money itself is certainly a resource, as our economist friends will tell us. The economy is organized in such a way that all of us work with money to achieve our goals in our lifetime.

But money is not the only resource we can employ to achieve our lives' desired goals. We have another resource – available to us, our time. We can employ or use our time to achieve our goals without worrying about money.

Another resource we have available to us is our physical effort and our intellectual effort, and even our artistic effort. These efforts are not only in terms of our time for these activities, but in terms of labor we put in or skill we possess and use.

The lesson we need to learn is we do not always pursue our lives and seek to earn money and money alone. We can employ our time as an investment of a non-monetary nature. We can work on physical, intellectual, or artistic pursuits, all for their own sake, with no evaluation in monetary terms.

In the world of the 21$^{st}$ century, we have another new resource at our command – technology and platforms that technologies offer to us. Instead of physically roaming the world, we can roam the virtual roads made available to us by technologies of communication with our fellow citizens. We can turn ourselves into gurus without leaving our homes, with the remote yet direct access to the world granted to us by 21st century technology.

# EMPLOY ALL RESOURCES – MONEY ALONE NOT TO DOMINATE

When we employ our resources, any of these resources, we can count their monetary value, or we just ignore the monetary value, as most of us do, and rightly so. We pursue our lives the way we wish to, employing our resources with the sole aim of being happy with our lives – not just our lifestyles but our life's content as well. We do not let money dominate all our decisions; we do not let money define our very own idea of happiness. We traverse two paths at the same time, in the monetary world and non-monetary world, by following whatever is the right path at any given time. We live in two economies – two worlds of money-driven economics and our own personal economics.

In the views of economists, who rigorously pursue the money-based economics, it is relevant to attribute equivalent monetary value to our time or our effort or our skills or our knowledge and count these inputs as costs, to be able to work with their cost-benefit analysis in monetary terms. For example, they would like to attribute a monetary value to the work done at home by your spouse!

Then there are some odd jobs pursued by some of us. Take the women in the oldest profession in the world. How do they make their decisions? Rationally? Only for money? Professional economists call this approach "freakonomics" as they believe still in their monetary economics, still assume that we take our life's decisions only in monetary terms, all of us - even the sex workers also decide in monetary terms; they lend their bodies to earn money and seek happiness with more money. Do they really? We must ask.

Professional economists continue to hold that, whether we are looking at people who employ their knowledge and skills, or practice the sex working profession, we still seek monetary benefit, computed in money terms, which, in their view is being "rational" enough to work towards the maximum benefit – only and finally in terms of money only. If we have more money, we will be happier, no matter how we earn money.

So, in effect, traditional economists are in denial mode as far as non-monetary economy is concerned. They ignore the non-monetary economy and economic decision makers, who in their opinion, are being "non-rational", non-profit seeking, as they pursue their non-monetary economics. In fact, non-monetary economics exists and "non-rational" people like us are in the majority, as we make our economics and make our decisions in accordance with our own economics, nonmonetary economics. Asking us to count the work we do in the family is an insult to our wisdom, disrespect for our living outside the monetary economics rules. Asking us to put a monetary value to all our activities and count our costs and our benefits may be "rational" in the economists' view but ignores all the non-monetary economic decisions we take outside of the money-based economy.

Many times, at many stages in life, we do make, and we must make, our decisions outside the traditional economics framework of a money-driven economy. If we choose to be a musician, even though a bank job will be more paying, we are pursuing non-monetary economics, we are seeking happiness from music, not from the money earned from another job. We decide whether we prefer music over other possible occupations. And we must; that decision is our personal economic decision. That decision is taken as our preferred route to happiness; we do not believe that more money will always result in more happiness for us. We can be happier with less money, too!

# MEASURE NONMONETARY BENEFITS AS WELL AS MONETARY BENEFITS

What is true of the costs side of their economics is also true of their benefits side of the cost-benefit framework. The professional economists try to measure all our benefits in monetary terms only. They try to count our benefits when measurable in monetary terms and ignore benefits we seek when they do not fit into the monetary valuation exercise. Work at home, work at a charity, work at collective social service, are all decisions for which conversion to monetary terms, monetary benefits does not serve any useful purpose for us at our personal level.

Fortunately for us, we can ignore the professional economists and their monetary cost versus benefits valuation framework.

So, what are the non-monetary benefits we seek?

We expect services when needed by us. We expect simple joy of togetherness with someone. We may expect acceptance as a member of our community, to be part of it. These outcomes are what make us happy, and we pursue them without any contamination of monetary translation of the benefits we seek. We treat our family or friends in these nonmonetary lifestyles, and do not wish to insult them by trying to attribute monetary values to their living with us and seeking to maximize their support just to benefit more in money terms.

To learn to live happily, we pursue both frameworks of economics - one driven by the "science" of economics and the other driven by our own personal economics.

So let us now go to our personal economics.

# THE PERSONAL ECONOMICS FRAMEWORK

The simplified economic framework of the science of economics tells us to count our costs and benefits and net gains. We will use it to set our personal economic rules about how we wish to live in the money-driven economy, and with looking at how we wish to live in the non-money-driven economy, both applying the cost/benefit/net gain framework. We may choose the higher paying job from two options open to us, monetary return – wages – being easy enough to "count". We may also "count" our "net gain" in non-monetary terms by putting a value on the happiness derived from a job well-liked.

But personal economics itself has a framework that we need to implement to set our rules. There are financial economists who help us with a framework that considers what we can do with money, an approach that tells us to mind the six actions that we can take and guides us on how to take the right decisions – earning, spending, saving, investing, withdrawing investments and sharing or giving away our savings or resources.

We purse both frameworks – the cost/benefits framework where we use money as a resource to seek some benefits, as assumed by the economists, and we also pursue the personal economics framework and use non-monetary resources to earn, spend, save or invest money, and withdraw money or non-monetary resources from our reserves when we need it or when we simply want to give it away.

Our personal economics framework can be used in both ways, one, where we still use money as the primary resource to count our costs and benefits and the six steps of personal economic decisions, and two, while dealing with our other personal resources besides money. Here, we do not count costs and benefits, do not seek returns from our investments. Do not translate all costs and benefits in money terms.

In the same manner, we may not plan to save only money as a resource, as a cost, as savings, nor do we seek to obtain benefits in terms of money alone. We try to earn, spend, save, invest, or withdraw investments in terms other than money, in terms of all our personal resources. Our time may be given, or our service or skill offered, our knowledge shared; these are our personal resources that we may use, without monetary count.

# Personal Economics with Money

What can we do with money?

Earn it.

In the monetary economy that we inhabit, we need to earn money. Without earning money, we cannot survive. We cannot buy all the goods and services we need to live happily.

Spend it.

We work on earning money to enable us to spend it. We need to spend money to obtain whatever we need to be able to live and live happily.

Save it.

We may not always be in a position to earn money either through disability or inadequate income due to general economic conditions, for example. In this case, our Personal Economics with Money ends here, unfortunately. To provide for that eventuality we need to save some money for use in future, whenever possible, as we need to "spend" our savings in future.

Invest it.

If you have been fortunate enough to have saved some money, the saved money cannot be kept idle under the mattress or in a bank. You need to invest the money saved so you can get some return on it and be able to use in future not just the saved amount but also the accumulated returns.

Withdraw it.

We cannot just keep our investments and marvel at them. We invest so we can use it someday to fund our expenses and to cover our spending. We need to withdraw money at the right time when we need to spend it in future.

Give it away.

If we have amassed money that is well beyond our spending needs, we need to consider different options of using "excess" money - giving it away to someone who needs it; or giving it away to our children on our death. But we can also consider giving it away to charity to sustain those unfortunate people who need but do not have money. It depends on your moral economics and concern for your children.

# Chapter Five

# PRACTICING THE ECONOMICS OF LIFE

Now let us understand the earning part of our economics of life.

# The Book of Earning

What is Earning?

What do you earn? How do we measure income?

How much do we need to earn?

Can we ignore money as the measure of happiness?

Why do we need to earn money?

How to earn income?

Working For Yourself

Part Time Work

Early Retirement

Working Without Money

Barter - Exchanging Goods for Goods

Exchanging Services for Services

Exchange of Community Work for Community Work

Creating Mutually Helpful, Self-Reliant and Egalitarian Communities

# What is Earning?

You earn income. Income is the reward for your work, the fruit of your labor.

For the science of economics, income is earned in the form of money received in return for work done by us.

For the economics of life, income may be earned in any form of reward that the earner finds of value – respect, recognition, or simply personal satisfaction.

In life, we may follow both the economics models – that of the science of economics – costs versus benefits, and that of the economics of life – earning, spending, saving, investing, withdrawing, and sharing and using up all that we saved and invested.

Earning is a concept of the economics of life. The science of economics effectively assumes that you earn only monetary income, since only monetary income can be measured and dealt with by economic scientists. In fact, you earn much more than money. You can earn respect, and warmth, and all kinds of non-monetary help. All that you earn goes to enriching your life, while the economists assume that only monetary income enriches your life.

Only you can "measure" your income and decide whether it is sufficient reward for your work or livelihood. Economists presume to decide for you what level of income is sufficient for you; even politicians decide for you; they cannot, however, decide what income "you" need and is "sufficient" for you, so ignore them, and you value your life and your work yourself, you decide yourself what income level is sufficient for you.

As you decide what level of income is sufficient for you, you may believe or be told that sufficient income means "enough" income that will satisfy all your needs. Surely, we need to be mindful of our needs as we determine what income level is needed for us. Yet this evaluation process is doomed to failure. Our needs are a moving goalpost, constantly going up, with new needs stepping in as we earn enough to satisfy our old needs. The sad truth is that no level of income is enough to satisfy all our needs. It is when we feel that we have earned enough to provide for most of our personal needs that level of income is sufficient for us.

There are some obvious guidelines to determine what is barely sufficient, or what is desirably sufficient.

Yes, we have to avoid starvation and have enough money to satisfy our hunger, the hunger of our dependent family; and this minimum earning has to be in money terms.

But let us not forget to add to the monetary rewards the nonmonetary rewards that we earn.

Let us remember that we can and need to generate earnings not just to satisfy our current needs but also to satisfy our future needs when we may not be earning or earning enough.

Let us also remember that there are people who devote themselves to earning for others as well as for themselves; they may be running a charity or an old age community, or simply by being a donor occasionally. This is indeed a noble way of earning, for others. And in this case, no level of income is "sufficient". There are also the donors who have earned enough and actually set up a foundation to support causes they care for, sufferers from some major disease or victims of a natural calamity. But even as a small-time donor, you may want to earn as much as you are capable of earning and use any surplus to support the earnings of those who do not earn enough to satisfy even their basic needs.

The science of economics does not cover your definition of sufficient income, nor the earnings for others. So, the economists measure only your own monetary needs and income, according to their professional definition of what constitutes sufficient or required income level for all. There is a class of economists who propagate the UBI – Universal Basic Income that they recommend the Government must support and give out to the needy. They can help manage the economy in a way that helps all of us earn a minimum income to satisfy our minimum needs as defined by them, of course in monetary terms and according to their definition of a basket of minimum needs. While framing these economic policies, they ignore us as masters of our own lives, who decide our own personal economics and our own earning that is enough for us.

Our own earning philosophy, our overall philosophy of life, define our economics of life.

- How to earn the things that we care about for our lives.
- What kind of rewards do we want to earn.
- How to measure our non-monetary as well as monetary earnings.
- How much do we need to earn.
- How do we go about taking our economic decisions.

The science of economics measures your income in terms of money. But the economics of life measure income in terms of happiness derived by way of money or by way of other forms of rewards for work performed.

Given our own philosophy of life, all of us do not derive happiness from the same set of rewards, and each of us can decide the set of measures from which we derive happiness and measure our earnings in terms of derived happiness.

Let us stick to this personal decision-making process, ignore the science of economics, use our freedom from the jailer – money.

Remember that we are in an economic prison and money is our jailer.

The way we have organized our civilized societies, we must learn to live in the economy and obey the rules of money.

So, money cannot be ignored. But money matters to the extent it can buy happiness, not more. Would you continue a "disliked" but well-paid job and remain unhappy? Or look for other options even with less wages or salary, but being happy? Would you give up your love for painting or sculpture with no guarantee of income, and choose a salaried job that sees a credit into your bank account every month?

Money itself can also give you unhappiness. That is why money is not of central importance. Happiness is. Our life matters. We must keep alive even in our prison. The activity or job is a must have condition in the money-driven economy; but the job content is at least as important as the money it brings into your pockets. Do you know that there are people who have "lots" of money but are unhappy with the amount of time required just to manage their wealth?

True, in the world of money, you will have to earn and depend on money. But you can also inhabit a whole new economy with non-monetary resources and measure your income not only in money but also in other rewards that give you happiness.

That income level is sufficient for you which buys you enough happiness, not just enough goods and services. It is your money and your happiness, not someone else's, not the economists' happiness. You decide the threshold of what is enough for you.

Economics tells us that you need to earn money to be able to spend it to buy various goods and services needed to live. But we also know that we want to buy the goods and services not only to be able to live but also to maintain a certain lifestyle that will make us happy.

Will the basket of goods and services proposed by the economists make us happy?

Here comes the economics of life. Only we can decide why we need and want to earn money. Further, we also know that we can earn other rewards for our work, rewards that buy us or give us happiness – rewards like recognition, respect, rest, or recreation. Measure your happiness in these and other non-monetary rewards that make you happy, or satisfied, or contented.

We need to earn both money and non-monetary rewards to be happy.

What is important to know is that, in the economic prison we inhabit, we need to earn before we can spend money. But in our personal sphere, we do not need to earn or work to earn other resources. There are some resources already given to us – time, for example. Certain skills or knowledge for example. These personal resources we can "spend" even before we "earn." We can first spend these personal resources to earn other non-monetary rewards, reversing the monetary economic prison rules.

We work on earning money to spend it later, but we can also spend our personal resources first to earn other rewards later. We may be happy to earn other forms of reward - recognition, respect, or simply happiness.

We also need to remember that we may go for the option of earning, not spending and keeping the rewards in a basket for future use to spend.

# HOW TO EARN INCOME?

To earn income, you can work for some other person or entity.

Remember, if you work for someone and if you earn your income in money, your income is someone else's expense. What you earn, the other person spends. So, while you will want to maximize your income, your employer would want to minimize his expense. Compensation causes conflict in work relationships.

Your employer might see you as a problem to deal with. Since his expense is measured in money, he would want you to make him more money with your help than what he spends on you. That is why working for someone else for money bedevils human relationships.

If you wish to avoid the conflict inherent in working for someone else in monetary compensation, compare being employed by someone else to a situation where you do not work for someone else or work for other things than money. That gives you another option – to earn income by working for oneself.

If you work for yourself, you do not feel you are exploiting yourself. Your earning as a worker does not become your expense, as it would be for your employer. So, there is no tension, no conflict in self-employment. And you pay yourself more than money. You can be happy with what you are doing. You can pay yourself in happiness, not just in money. This is ideal—you need money to buy happiness, so if you can buy happiness directly by working for yourself, that is the best option. If you can pay yourself and buy yourself happiness, what more can you ask for?

If you choose to be self-employed, you can set all your work-related conditions yourself, including not getting paid in money but in kind or even in services you provide to others. Thus, you can be happy in both the worlds, monetary economy, and non-monetary economy.

Unfortunately, all of us do not have the ability to employ ourselves and earn enough to be able to live on the earnings. Hence, it is inevitable that most of us work for others. At least so far, we have not found a way of creating a society where all its members are self-employed.

There is a middle way between working for others and working for yourself.

You can divide your active time, giving a part to working for others and the rest to working for oneself. That way you earn an essential amount of money, and devote your personal time to service, even working for money but for yourself, on projects that appeal to you, that you like, that you find happiness from.

Combine the scientific economics during active mornings of your life, get a part time reprieve from the money-driven economic prison, and combine it with a self-chosen vocation, following the economics of your life, in the afternoons.

If it is not possible for you to find part-time work that satisfies your monetary earning needs, you can choose a second midway – work full-time but stop when you have earned enough and move to working on your own, following your economics of life, on what may be paying vocation. Payment may be in monetary terms or non-monetary terms, immediate or deferred. The goal is to work on projects close to your heart, what gives you happiness. With early retirement, you stop working as a prisoner of economics governed by money, and start working on projects outside the rational, wealth generation economic goal. You go directly to work and earnings terms of your choice.

There is, however, the need for you to choose part-time work or early retirement with full understanding of the monetary economy and personal economics. You need to judge whether your monetary earnings will be enough when you take the decision to choose part-time work or early retirement. And you need to understand your own preferences for the work that gives you happiness. That is the meaning of what is now called "work-life balance."

If you work for someone else but do not accept money or the equivalent, you can avoid the main element of conflict in the relationship. The question is: While it is greatly beneficial for your employer if you work for him without getting paid or paid in money, why would you work without getting paid? You will do it if you have sufficient money of your own, so work is only for your enjoyment or for someone else's benefit as in the case of charity. This does not mean you have to be very wealthy to have this luxury; even as someone who has earned and saved and invested enough money or non-monetary rewards, you too can choose this option. It depends on your philosophy of life, your monetary resources and whether you consider them "sufficient".

If you have sufficient money, it is best to prefer to work for others without accepting money. You would be happy. There will be fewer conflicts arising from paid work. And there will be more mutual respect among human beings. After all, this respect that you get is also your earning.

"Less developed" societies of the past and even in the present were/are organized less as money-driven economies, but more as non-monetary resources-based societies, accepting non-monetary "currencies." They benefit from mutually supportive social organization. We work without monetary reward, and others work for us without monetary rewards.

It is possible, even for us, even within the money-driven society, to work without money, which will mean the society would benefit through more mutually supportive relationships within itself and be less dependent on others.

Today far too many people work for money and for themselves, though they do not need to keep earning. They can in fact keep earning not for themselves but to share their wealth with others in need. Society will not only be happy but also be far more economically productive, since earnings will not be idle as savings and investments, but will be employed and spent, albeit on others.

With mutually supportive work relationships both the donor and the beneficiary gain personal satisfaction and happiness. Those following this social set up are out of the money race, the race to keep working and amassing wealth, and amassing more wealth than others. The society would be valuing more your personal strengths than your wealth. Money will not bedevil social relationships, as in the case of the employer-employee relationship. We will be happier that way: having provided for our own needs and supporting others.

Let us remember that, even if we do not earn money by choice, we can still be paid in terms of respect or recognition, or gratitude of the beneficiary of our work, who may pay us back in any form of reward in future when we need, may be money, may be unpaid help and support in exchange of our past work without money.

Earning by working without immediate reward in money amounts to postponing our earnings into the future. If we do not need immediate reward, we can work and not look for immediate reward. Again, choice of this option depends upon your situation where you consider your present income and past savings to be "sufficient". It also depends upon your need to accept unpaid work with the goal being acquiring some education or skills – as in the case of students.

Even in this case, let us remember that we still need some money to be able to live, spend on our immediate needs, unless you have sufficient money for the present, either your own or your supporters' like your parents or other funding sources. Unfortunately, not many of us have enough money to live happily and then work for others without being paid in money. Hence, we must consider other options.

# Barter – Exchanging Goods for Goods

Before the invention of money, past societies and their markets worked with a "barter" mechanism. I may need some goods and have other goods to offer in exchange; if we can agree on the quantity of how many goods can be exchanged for how many other goods.

Where goods are exchanged for goods, problems associated with money are avoided. Thus, monetary inflation in the prices of goods becomes irrelevant. We can continue to hold the ratio of goods bought to goods sold, which is effectively the "price" which depends upon the available supply of what goods we need as opposed to supply of our goods. Inflation means more of our goods are asked for in exchange for other goods. We have to match goods to buy with goods to sell, which can become a difficult exercise. Barter markets are therefore limited.

In the world today, bartering of goods has become unmanageable as manufacturing of goods has been globalized and physical caravans of goods taking them for barter with other goods at other locations are no longer possible. Most of the goods can be bought only with money. Hence, we need money as the common measure of exchange of goods we need to purchase. Think of your wanting to buy a piece of furniture against some fruits you can sell! Impossible exchange, without valuation in money. Money separates the purchases from sales, as each type of goods is valued independently of each other. Furniture has a price in money; so do the fruits.

A small window for bartering still exists in rural areas, geographically small, where inhabitants can exchange some goods for other goods, mostly local products, on a reciprocal basis, thereby limiting the role of money. Vegetable or fruit markets can work on a barter basis. Many villages of the poorer countries still operate this limited barter system. The professional economists will regard these consumers in the barter economy dismissively, as their barter is not captured and measured by monetary economics.

Even in rich countries, there is now some opposition to globalized supply chains, where large corporations supply goods globally, of course for money. Localized production and exchange of localized goods is sought to be brought back, a decision that values our lives, not our money. It is an economics of life decision. Ask the French farmers or winegrowers! They want to be happy with local products, even if costlier in money terms, than the globalized equivalents sold by multinational marketplaces. Indeed, some globalization can be replaced by local markets.

In the world today, barter-based goods markets are few and far between, and money facilitates exchange of goods, by independently valuing each type of goods. The Barter model is ancient but its application in the 21$^{st}$ century needs to be expanded to services as well as goods. This option involves working for those who work for us, now or later. What this means is that we employ the services of others and in return we provide our services to them. It is a barter of services.

Services are generally provided from one person to another and are localized. It is possible for one person to barter his services with others without involving an exchange of money. The age-old example of barter of services is probably domestic help, where cleaning and maintenance services of someone are used to provide financial services in return. For example, the medical or food needs of the domestic help may be provided by the user of his services.

Even in modern society it is possible to organize small communes where most of the services are exchanged for other services and people may either work for others and be paid in services or be self-employed and sell some services in return for others' services. Israel's Kibbutz are a live example. Medical protection services may be assured on a co-operative basis among the participants in the communal arrangement. Co-operative farming is another possibility.

Where work is exchanged for work, problems associated with money are avoided. Thus, inflation in the prices of goods or services becomes irrelevant. Normally, people are more respectful of others when it comes to using their time, knowledge, and services. Besides, we have the option of quitting the arrangement of the barter of services if we feel that we are not getting enough services in return.

The principal lesson for us is that we need not become a slave to money, we can work outside the money-driven economy, even without going to the mountains or the bush, and use non-monetary measures and rewards. We can resort to barter or exchange of services for services, bypassing the money-driven economy.

Ancient economies were indeed organized for barter, not only the physical barter of goods, but also barter of services and mutual exchange of services; the ancient economies simply did not have the jobs as we look for now. They had to have members of the society either in self-employment or in barter arrangements at personal level, or community level.

Yet we need to recognize that even in ancient societies, there were inconveniences resulting from dependence only on barter for goods or for services. Hence, past societies felt the need for a measure of exchange – money in one form or another.

Even this limitation of barter-based societies can be partly overcome by governments and the community itself. We can organize, for example, financial services exchange at a commune level. Local financing solutions can be put in place to ensure that the immediate needs of its members are funded and fulfilled by the financial services exchange, so avoiding the mismatch of timing of our need for services we need now and their availability on a barter basis. Local economies would be regulated by local authorities to be as self-sufficient as possible for as many goods and services as possible, and the remaining balance of goods and services can be given by the larger economic units or governments. The role of the money-driven economy will be limited to the commune government level, while the community members belong to an economy based on the economics of life.

# Creating Mutually Helpful, Self-Reliant and Egalitarian Communities

While we cannot escape fully from our economic prisons, we can be granted a parole to walk out partly and from time to time, to breathe fresh air and not worry about Money the Jailer. We can create communities as an answer to finding happiness outside the prison.

The social exchanges of services, both person to person, and community to community, are the ideal vehicles to ensure everyone and all members of a community get to enjoy the services, whether they have enough money to spend on buying the services or not.

Solely money-driven exchanges create inequality where those who can, manage to earn a lot of money in excess of their need, whereas others who cannot, do not manage to earn enough money to pay for the services they need but cannot afford.

On the other hand, service exchange-driven communities ensure equality at least in terms of community inhabitants having access to all or most of the services they need, irrespective of whether they have enough money to purchase these services or not. They will pay for the use of our services in exchange for the services they can and will provide. How about some vegetables for haircut services! They earn and spend the non-monetary but socially important rewards- sometimes money but many times in other rewards that can be shared with others in the community. We get our daily needs from people who were grateful to us for services rendered by us in the past. We can be recognized as a commune-level service provider as a medical doctor, eligible for other services, for example.

Creating such service-exchange-based economies ought to be and can be the policy task of the regulators, governments, and community leaders. Their goal will be to encourage service exchanges and organized and equitable distribution of services. There needs to be no element of compulsion in the social organization, as, for example, in communist economies where inhabitants are forced to give up individual ownership of assets – monetary or non-monetary. The regulators do not decide what services will be provided by whom.

Their goal is to encourage creative social processes that ensure equal access to services everyone needs, without the regulators deciding which services everyone needs – the community leaders and members themselves who decide what services they want in the community pot and shared by all whenever needed. Housing, clothing, and food would be basic needs to cover. Other services like medical help can be in the communal pot as well.

The creation of service-driven local communities is not an unrealistic Utopian project as it may seem to be. Villages, their inhabitants, and local leaders can build working communes even in today's money-driven world. It is possible to expand the communal arrangements to many services, taking them out of the money-based economy and putting them in the to-be-shared basket of the commune; the goal would be to assure their availability to all inhabitants.

Agrarian villages are a good example. They will be good vehicles to implement self-reliant communities. Voluntary groups like *Médecins Sans Frontières* can provide specific services, in this case medical services; other groups can form sub-communities around other services in the commune. Israel's self-reliant Kibbutz is another good model.

We need to recognize that we cannot create a Utopian vehicle where "all" services are available at each vehicle, group, village, or Kibbutz. The regulatory model of these "services Kibbutz" will be a two-level organization. Local services exchanges include as many services in the local pot as possible. The rest of the services are sourced from the outside – country or foreign entities. At some point, individuals or communes will need money and return to the larger entity – State – and the money-based economy. Services not provided by the smaller vehicle can be provided by the larger vehicle. Money can come from State Budgets for the grant to the commune, or the commune may have some surplus money or services. At the individual level, Social Security would be used to support the local communes where their role or available means end.

Such services exchanges working with common services to be shared without being money for money transactions is like walking out of money-driven economic prison, outside the scope of money as the jailer.

Money-driven social exchanges can remain in place, but all exchanges will not be in terms of money. Policy makers and economists can manage money-driven economies. But non-money based, and service exchanges-driven economies can be created by communities themselves and regulated by local governments.

The money-driven conflicts between one who earns money and one who gives the services can be lessened and confined to money-driven parts of the economies, while all non-money-based exchanges of community services are provided with equal respect and equal access for all and each member of the community. Corruption and cheating for money can be lessened if not eliminated; at least these money-driven anti-social behaviors can be confined to money-driven economies only, while communities control and punish such activities.

Earning money need not be a selfish activity but a need-based activity where money is seen as a means of exchange, not a means to acquire and hoard "wealth" in money. We human beings are capable of reducing the impact of money on our lives, of identifying and isolating those who seek to amass money and hold power over us. If we cannot control them individually, the communities to which we belong can control them and deal with them. We do not need to be dependent on money for all our needs, and so earn community points to be exchanged with others. We can make the money earners irrelevant beyond a certain threshold.

Let us get out of the belief that only "money" can be earned. We can go for "barter" of goods or services with others, either individually or through our self-created communes. We value "community points – loyalty points" and be happy to live without earning money dictating our lives. We can now address the next step – spending our money earned or non-monetary resources earned.

# THE BOOK OF SPENDING

# Why Spend?

The point of earning an income is to acquire the ability to spend. The purpose of spending is to acquire the means to satisfy our life's needs.

Spending is a necessity. To satisfy our needs and to achieve a lifestyle we desire.

In economic science earning is followed by spending, and saving the money is the next step after spending. In the economics of life, we have the freedom to earn and save, not spend or spend in future; we will see later how.

In our economic prisons, we must spend time on work in order to earn our daily bread. In the money-driven economic prisons that we live in, we need to spend money on purchasing goods and services that are available only by spending money.

We do not spend because we earn. Whether we earn or not, we have to spend money to purchase the goods and services we desire. That is why it does not matter how much we earn; we must spend. We spend because we desire goods and services that we think we need. Our level of income does explain often why and what we desire beyond our basic needs.

It is our spending needs that will define what we need to earn; our spending needs are independent of our earning level.

We can spend only what we earn. Living inside our economic prison, we can only spend money, as it is the only common currency that other community members – fellow prisoners, accept. Money is essential to earn so we can spend it on acquiring all the goods and services we need to satisfy our needs.

Money, otherwise a common currency all over the world, is not the same in all countries and economies. We need to exchange the currency we earn, or have with us, for the accepted currency of the country we live in, the economy we inhabit.

Usually, we are paid in the currency of the country we live in, obviating the need to change the currency. As long as we live in an economy where we can spend the monetary currency we earn, or have, we can purchase goods and services we need. If we earn in a currency that is different from our local currency, we need to exchange that foreign currency for our local currency. This currency exchange facility may or may not be available in our economic prison by its rules. Governments make the rules of the monetary currency that you are allowed to earn, acquire, and exchange.

If you live in a country free of the currency exchangeability regulations, you are fortunate. If you acquire a foreign currency that your country of residence does not accept, it is useless in your hands.

That is why you can spend only what you earn or acquire. That means you can spend only your own local currency, acceptable as a medium of exchange within your economic prison. You may spend it in different modes – for example a loaded credit card, but how you spend – bills or "plastic" cards, the designated or permissible currency will still be the local currency. When we think of money, we mean the legal tender – using the greenback or the credit or debit cards is about how we spend, spending still being in legal tender.

You need to acquire the type of money you are allowed to spend. You will have to go hungry if you have, if you try to purchase goods or services you need, with an Indian rupee, in Europe or the U.S., unless you first exchange rupees into euros or dollars before you can buy whatever you need.

You can spend not only what you earn, but what currency in which you earn. If you are fortunate enough to earn in your local currency for goods and services you spend in other countries say euros or dollars, if other countries allow you to earn your local currency, you will have no exchange problem. But many countries have rules against foreigners being allowed to earn in a currency that is their local currency, but a foreign currency to them. Further, the rules may permit you to exchange your currency of earnings into your local currency, but many countries may not allow that option as well.

You can spend only your local currency, or money exchangeable to your local currency, the currency of the economy you inhabit. So, count your spending only in your own currency, convert your spending in any other currency to your own base currency and ignore how and where you spend the money.

Note also that how you spend money has nothing to do with the problems and appeal of "bartering". We still inhabit the money-driven economy and spend "money" in whatever form we use; money still facilitates our purchases and sales with no need to barter.

How we can spend the non-monetary money-equivalent is about the Economics of Life – we shall see later.

The biggest challenge facing us in our personal economics is to match our monetary spending power with our earnings in money.

As we know, we determine our spending level independently of our earning power. Hence, the reality is that our income rarely matches our spending. Some of us earn more than we spend. Some of us earn less. That is because our income depends on our ability to contribute to our employer's income or ability to provide a valuable product or service to our customer, at least in a free labor market.

The result is a society where we get paid in money according to our ability to deliver value to our employer or to our customer.

If we earn more than what we spend, it means our needs are fully satisfied by spending and we end up with surplus income. Then, we have to decide what we ought to do with the surplus income; we will address this question in later chapters.

If we are not fortunate enough to earn sufficient money to be able to spend on all our requirements, the economics of our life stop here. We will have to go with unsatisfied needs or may become dependent on someone else to fund our shortage.

Who will fund our shortage of income? One way is through social support.

The communists and socialists have tried to intervene by regulation to ensure that we get income in accordance with our needs rather than our abilities. The system has not really worked except to a limited extent, because all of us are self-centric – we want and like to earn according to our ability, even if it is more than our needs; otherwise, we feel short-changed; we may even get discouraged from contributing our full set of "abilities".

The earlier suggestion of considering a barter of goods and services still stands; it helps us if the exchange is possible in practice. But we have come far too away from only barter economies which have to be money-based to facilitate for you and me purchases and sales, using money as an intermediary currency. That is why we need to and generally like to get paid in money, and then have the freedom to spend it, rather than get paid in services or products to the extent we need them.

The tricky question for the governments is determining what level of income would be considered sufficient for all of us, what level of spending would be considered as needed by all of us, what level of needs they ought to satisfy. Given our diverse needs, what needs may be considered as reasonable, "minimal" requirements for the government to satisfy?

Communists consider housing, food, and clothing as the minimum needs to be satisfied. Even those needs are not easy to satisfy, as governments mostly lack the resources for implementation of the social support that they need to plan and make arrangements for. Then there is the question of corruption in the implementation of the communist system; the rulers reserve for themselves the best of all available resources – bigger housing space, better food, or clothing.

Governments in the post-communist world, the democratic countries, now recognize that the whole populace does not have uniform needs, and it is more difficult for the governments to provide directly the needs of all. As a result, the governments now also revert to money as the basis of means to satisfy our needs. They practice two options, both in the money-based economies.

The first solution is to decide what common "social services" they can and do provide. Here the working example is the medical expense support applicable to all. As we need to spend on getting medical help, the governments provide reimbursements through medical insurance or directly. Beneficiaries are all of us, the rich as well as the poor or needy. There is no eligibility criterion of our income level.

As to the second solution, the governments now have also been experimenting with providing to all its nationals what is called "universal basic income." This is the monetary equivalent of what they judge to be the basic cost of living in the economy they manage. They simply dole out the cash to the needy, those who either do not have any income, or are short of income. The target is the relatively low-income or poor segments of the society, with income level threshold defined to keep the rich out of the social support system.

Unlike the communists who sought to take on the responsibility to house, feed and clothe all its population, the democratic governments today aim to provide a social safety net for those who do not earn minimum income to be able to live reasonably. And they use the money as the vehicle, whether to provide social services or the universal basic income.

The calculation of the required basic universal income figure is left to the economists, as national income accountants.

There are problems, however, not just with estimating the universal basic income. First there could be corruption even under this system. Even if honestly administered, there is the challenge of identifying and validating the real needy who could be considered eligible for government dole outs. In countries with vast, poverty-stricken populations, many may not even be aware of their eligibility. Then, there are those who may not be eligible but manage to show themselves as being. This is still the best of the social safety net we have, unfortunately only in the case of just a few countries. Workable experience based, need based, money-based systems need to be developed and implemented in each country with their circumstances taken care of.

# Spending More to Satisfy More Needs

The real problem of people not having sufficient spending power is that nearly all of us go on increasing our requirements and needs after we get what is considered the minimum required income.

Ultimately, what to spend, how much to spend, are personal decisions. We need to arrive at a conclusion about our needs and requirements, at what level of income we can control ourselves and come to accept that level as being enough to satisfy our needs. Spending must relate to income.

Here is the problem of personal economics of our own – how much we earn or can earn, how much to spend, how to fund any shortage, and when do we reach the conclusion that we have enough to spend. Here also steps in our greed. As soon as we earn what is enough, we want to increase our needs. No amount of earning, no amount of support is enough to satisfy our ever-increasing needs. The spending power we have is always less than what we want.

So, the first major reason why our earning is not enough to allow us to have the spending power we want, is that we do not consider, or feel, that our earning is "enough."

# Matching Spending with Earnings – Spending Less by Reducing Your Needs

Here, the ideal solution to the problem of lack of spending power comes from the teachings of Buddha and Gandhi – to reduce our needs and seek less income. Buddha identified desire as the source of unhappiness, so he said let us reduce our desires and wants, so we will be happy with what we have. Unfortunately, this seemingly ideal solution has not been followed by most of us. Even after centuries/millennia after Buddha, we have gone on increasing our desires, needs and requirements. Our income is larger, our spending is larger and so is our shortage as our needs have expanded.

The solution of reducing our needs has been practiced by Christian monks, and Hindu sanyasis, and Moslem faqirs and other religious orders; so, we know that it can be done – reducing our needs to the minimum. Yet they are in a small minority. The rest of us go on increasing our wants and desires, not reducing them. In fact, economists aim at constant growth in our needs and spending level, thus encouraging money-based, consumerist economies. Buddha 2500 years ago, Gandhi in the 20th century, have failed to stem the appeal of more needs, more income, more spending, except perhaps for Christian monks, Hindu Sanyasis or Moslem faquirs, unfortunately a microscopic minority.

With our compensation in money aligned to what our employer or customer thinks is "correct" and in line with our contribution to his needs, the society organized around money is not always ideal and just, where our employer or customer actually does pay us what we deserve in accordance with our ability. So, the level of income we earn also depends on the level of exploitation that exists in the society we form part of. This is the second reason income does not always match our spending.

Again, the social and economic reformers have tried to eliminate or reduce economic exploitation, with some success but not always. Modern governments try to achieve the purpose through regulation of employers. Reformers try to unite us as consumers of products and services. On the other hand, industry and trade associations try to protect the interests of employers. In the end, in an environment fraught with all these economic and social power struggles, only you can help yourself from being exploited.

We generally get exploited because of our own lack of awareness, or inability or unwillingness to ask for what we deserve. Some of us have a stronger ability to ask for more – more payment than what some of us others get for the same product or service, or more wages for the same work. This is the third reason our income may not match our needs or abilities. We may be relatively weaker than others, so we get exploited. There are differences among us – not just in level of needs or abilities, but in the ability to demand money for work or for service or product sold.

As a result of all of us wanting to earn sufficient income, the best we have is our prison – an economy, a society where we get paid in money according to our ability to deliver value to our employer or to our customer and are left to ourselves to decide whether what we are being paid is "sufficient" for us. What we earn in terms of our ability may or may not be enough to match our income to our spending needs.

How do we match our earnings with our spending needs?

The economic solution is to work towards constantly increasing our income through growth, so we can support a constantly growing set of needs. This is the acquisitive, logical, scientific solution proposed by economists. It is based on the assumption that all of us are driven by increasing needs, and in reality, also by increasing greed!

The second solution is proposed by religious and social reformers - work towards reducing your needs to match your income, being content with what you have. These economics are based on the assumption that we are capable of developing contentment and guiding our life more with contentment than with greed.

Indeed, certain individuals fall out of the scientific economist's world of growth and achieve happiness by matching their needs to their income. Remember our "limited" budgets as "students"? When some of us accepted a lower-paid job or activity because the nature of the work brought us happiness. We remain happier in a small house as opposed to a big one. We do not go for "gourmet" foods.

But we need not all turn into either saints or mendicants and paupers. We need not reduce our needs to subsistence level. However, we can moderate our needs, be content with the level of income we have, and keep our spending within the income level. This is possible, of course, only if we live in a society where we are not economically exploited, where our contentment does not become the sure source for someone else's greed to make money. This is also possible if all the other fellow beings do not base their lives on the economics of greed, while we try to live contented lives. Unfortunately, there are many people who seek to live by greed. What do we do then?

# From Greed to Contentment – and The New Economics of Life

We need to move from the economics of money to the economics of life, to our own economics. To be happier, of course.

It is possible for us to leave our economic prison on short term parole that our prisoner can grant to us. We go to a world that runs on other drivers than money.

Earning and spending "enough" is possible, of course, only if we live in a society where we are not economically exploited, where our contentment does not become the sure source for someone else's greed to make money. Unfortunately, if we face many of our fellow beings who live on acquisitions based on greed, or simply a desire to get ahead of others, not permitting others to live on contentment, we face the unfortunate fight between the good and the evil, the fight where the science of economics meets human psychology.

In the fight, the scientific economists have sided with the economics of greed and have been advising, successfully, the governments of the world on how to satisfy human greed. What we need is a rejection of this breed of scientific economists who pursue only money-based economics with constant growth as the goal – growth in monetary income and spending levels of all. What we need from the economists is support for unscientific but human economists who can make us happy and wealthy despite disavowing the economics of greed based on money alone. This is too big a challenge for the logical, quantitative-mathematically oriented, scientific economist. They measure only money and ignore our non-monetary economics.

The economists of the future will have to come from psychologists, social reformers, philosophers, and humanities students. Economists of the future will have to be religious preachers, preaching the new economic faith based on mutual trust, co-operation, and contentment. Only the new unscientific economist will be able to give us the knowledge and the secrets of achieving economic well-being without being greedy, without being driven by money alone, uniting personal economics with scientific economics.

Will the universities and the academicians they host bring about the emergence of a new brand of economists?

Until this new brand of human economists arrives, where do we look for guidance, what do we do?

In the money-based economy we inhabit, we can only spend money. But we know, by now, that in our personal economy, we can spend other earnings, too.

These money-based economies have effectively turned into economic prisons, where we are dependent on the rations accorded to us by the jailer, our income. What we have to spend is determined both by money available and the price we are required to pay for the goods and services. Price level is the same for all prisoners. Success in a money-driven activity ultimately means the ability to spend. Spending power is the basis of monetary economics.

Just metaphorically, many of us have learnt to get around the jailer, or even bribe the jailer, and spend more than other prisoners, because we manage to earn more than the others. Then there are others who have even bigger spending power than we do. Their rations are bigger than ours. We have to deal with this inequality in the prison.

If we derive our happiness only from money available for spending, our happiness can degenerate into unhappiness that other prisoners have bigger spending power than we do. But we should also know that we can expand our spending power by spending more than money while out on parole from jail – our personal resources.

Spending in the personal economy of life, we know that what matters is the spending power, not just monetary spending power.

How do we face this Economics of Spending Power?

We know that we can spend other resources we have. Our time. Our services. Our solidarity with fellow prisoners. These resources also help us acquire goods and services we need, though not immediately. We can and must spend all our resources, not just money.

Yet we ought to know that even these non-monetary resources can buy us many things in future, that we can cultivate these non-monetary resources to supplement our spending power. We can make our time. We can cultivate our skills and use them to spend our services. We can simply offer our sympathies and buy solidarity from others. And all that means that our spending power is not limited to money available for spending. We can create our own spending power by creating our non-monetary resources.

# CREATE A CARING AND SHARING SOCIETY

All of us have the right to be personally happy by spending not only our money but also the non-monetary resources we have available to spend. But we need to go beyond our own resources for our own happiness; we need to and can create our own economy, and our own society, where we can spend our time and effort and skills and sympathy for others, without any expectation to earn anything from those for whom we spend our non-monetary resources. In other words, we donate our resources now for the sake of the society and its members when in need. These people or others we may not even know will repay us in ample measure by spending their resources on us, their time, their effort, their services, their sympathies. We care for our fellow members of the society and share our resources with them when needed. Others will also promote a caring and sharing society by fulfilling our needs with their resources. And we will all be happy, collectively, not selfishly. Society will be happy.

Creating such a society does need some big plans or structure. Be the change you seek in others; this has been a teaching of the Gandhis of the world. Help others and they will return your help. Individuals create a caring and sharing society by their personal contributions and encouraging others to do the same.

A happy society is created by happy individuals. Back to Gandhi, and Buddha, and Christ – each of us must contribute to creation of a caring and sharing economy by us being caring and sharing.

We have seen that this caring and sharing society can also be a public goal where the governments help structure models like the Kibbutz or self-governing agrarian centers. But creation of such structures is not imperative, and we do not need to wait for the structures to be created. We can move on our own.

# The Book of Saving

## Why Save?

## Savings Define You

## Savings Matter in the Monetary Economy

## Savings In the Economics of Life

When your income is more than what you spend, the balance - excess income - is what you save. However, remember that you save money when your income is more than what you *can* spend or what you *want* to spend.

When you must save money because your income is more than what you *can* spend, you are rich. When you save money out of choice because you *want* to, you are a conservative person. Many people save money because of insecurity about the future, or concern for the future of their children or concern for their own old age. Some economically knowledgeable people save money because they expect to live on income from savings in the future. Some save because they expect inflation; they expect the value of their money/savings to decline in future.

When you save money because you do not need all your income, you are a contented person, because you can always spend more money – or you may get satisfaction in "saving" more, and more, money. But if you save money even when you need a part of your income, and then spend it on others, you are a benevolent person.

Pursuing the core theme of "scientific" economics - wealth accumulation through saving money, the current money-based economists cannot account for the contented or the benevolent persons who do not seek continuous wealth accumulation in money. The economic "science" does not know how to deal with "unscientific" economic decisions based on contentment or benevolence. Decisions like earning and spending but not saving money, or not seeking personal wealth accumulation, or giving their wealth away, are all anathema to professional economists; they cannot "count" such decisions and account for such decision makers. That is why economic advisors stop at the wealth accumulation phase after considering costs, benefits, and net gains. For them, producing "net" gains, saving money and accumulating wealth, are all that economics is about.

Let us accept then, that, for professional economists, "savings" matter only in a monetary economy. Let us remember that we live also in our own non-monetary economy as well. We ordinary human beings can, do and need to define and evolve our own economics based on contentment and benevolence – whether big time donations, or small amounts of charity to those in need. We need to go beyond producing wealth to using it for others. Economic science assumes that all of us want to go on saving money if we can, that we love money and wealth strongly enough to go on saving more and more. Economic science knows, understands, and deals with only those people who they assume have insatiable greed.

The concept of savings is inextricably tied to the concept of money. If we still lived in barter economies where no money was needed, no savings will be needed either. You could save some goods that could fetch you other goods in future. But then, these goods might have to be as good as money or currency such as gold that does not lose value with time and that continues to be acceptable to all for exchange of goods.

We the non-economists also have our own personal economics, our Economics of Life.

The point is that the monetary savings are useful to the extent that they enable you to buy goods and services in the future. The trouble is that, with your savings, you can buy goods and services in the future, but you cannot buy the future. Money saved today may help you fight future hardship, but your saving will not prevent the occurrence of future hardship. Life is independent of money. That is why money is needed in the first place. But money cannot control life. That is why life matters more than money. That is why economics matter less than life. That is why what ought to concern us are economics of life, not the science of economics that is independent of our lives.

# The Book of Investing

Why Invest?

From Savings to Investment – How and Where

Risks in Investing

Money Drives the Economy

Money Creates Unequal Wealth

We Can Create Other Kinds of Wealth

You earn money, spend part of it, and save the other part. Money saved has to be invested until spent again.

Investing means using money saved to generate more money, not keeping your savings idle.

But why convert savings to investments? Reason has to do with the nature of money-based economies. Money in hand today has much more value than the same money in the future. Money saved but not invested will lose value with price inflation, since its purchasing power will decline.

Spending money means using it to buy goods and services, now, at present. Saving money means you want to set aside some of your money to buy the same or better goods and services in the future. We want to retain the value of our savings at the same level as today. But the goods and services almost certainly will cost more money than today. Thus, your savings, left uninvested, will have less purchasing power than they do today. Money, and savings, lose value as time goes by.

The value of future money is the reason why the money not spent, and saved, has to be invested in a manner that gives us the ability to spend the savings in future, to have available to us the same goods and services we need in the future, when we may not be earning.

Money saved is also needed to protect our future, to have the savings available to us in the event of any future need, not necessarily goods and services, but to meet the circumstances that need money, too, such as illness, or family members' needs, such as education for our children or even grandchildren.

If you keep your savings in currency, under your mattress or in the cupboard, it does not help in holding your savings' spending power; you invest because you want to save your spending power at the same level as now at the time of saving.

Money invested is money made available by the savers to the borrowers or users of money.

Money may be lent to borrowers who promise to pay a return in terms of money. This form of investing is usually called lending, if our savings are lent directly to the borrower, with an agreement. Alternatively, we may invest in a debt instrument such as a bond indirectly from the stock market. Directly made loans cannot be recalled by us except as provided in the agreement, or by mutual consent. Debt securities we purchase from stock market are "tradeable", which means we can recover our money by selling the securities again through the stock market. Usually, debt securities have a maturity date – a date when the borrower must repay the full amount of our lending with interest if due. We can hold the securities until maturity or recall our loan or sell the bond in the market.

Money given by the borrower to the investor for the period of the use of the amount invested is called interest. Interest you receive may be at a fixed rate or at a floating rate. Interest may be paid once every quarter or six months or twelve months.

Besides the debt securities, in which case repayment of interest and principal amount of our lending is promised by the borrower, there is another type of investment we can make – through purchase of "equity" shares from the stock market. In this case, money is given, not lent, to users of money who promise to return your money as and when they earn more money from the use of your money. There is no "maturity date" on which the issuer of shares would repay the amount to investors. Usually, such investing means buying an "equity" interest in a corporation or even in an individual enterprise. Equity holders become part owners of the issuing entity. The equity instrument has a set price when issued. Its price then fluctuates on the market if the shares are "listed" and tradeable in the market. The price we pay for the purchase of shares is our cost; the price we get when we sell the security is the return of our investment, our gain or loss when compared to our cost price. What we need to note is that the repayment of an equity instrument is not guaranteed, nor even any return on the investment. Market price is based on the investors' views of what the "value" of the issuer entity is at any time. That is why equity instrument is called a risk instrument.

Money may thus be invested directly by lending or giving it to ultimate users through the public markets. However, if you as a saver find these forms of investments too complex to follow, as a further option, you as a saver may invest indirectly by keeping your money with financial intermediaries such as banks or mutual funds. Banks hold our funds in trust and guarantee the return of these funds; they turn around and invest our deposited funds either as loans to others or as earning securities, but any risk with funds so lent out is not for depositors/our account; banks guarantee our originally deposited funds and payment of interest on the deposits.

The other option of indirect investments is by savers buying shares of mutual funds. Mutual Funds hold our funds in trust and invest in a portfolio of financial securities, such investments being for our account and risk, as they invest on savers' behalf. This is unlike banks which invest at their own risk, not ours.

If you place your money in a bank, you retain the right to claim your funds back. You are sharing your money with the financial institution, for use in some productive part of the economy, you are not giving away your resources for good.

When you buy the equity shares of corporate entities, you are still sharing your resources with the share-issuing company, though the issuer of equity will not return your money directly, but you can find a buyer of your shares in the market.

When you buy insurance protection against certain risks, you pay a premium that insurance companies keep, and use the income to invest directly for them. You are guaranteed the sum assured, but not a full refund of your premium paid, as it becomes the revenue of the insurer.

You can entrust your money to mutual funds that invest in equity and debt securities but at your risk, the funds act as your money managers.

All these are ways to hold your savings and to invest either directly or indirectly through an intermediary. Each option comes with a different risk profile, but together they take your savings out from under the mattress! Why you should consider these investment routes is to make your savings productive and generate some income for you.

Where and how to invest is an area where you will find a vast number of investment experts and advisors willing to point to investment opportunities, ideas, and modes of investing.

Most of us lack the knowledge or time to find users of our money and return it later with more value. Hence, direct investments carry a risk that the savers make the wrong choices. Even if we go through investment advisors, ultimately, it is our own money that is at risk, not the advisors'.

Even in the case of indirect investments, for savers keeping money in banks involves taking a risk on the bank which invests on its own and guarantees the return of the savers' deposits on its own. Mutual funds on the other hand invest strictly on behalf of savers, at the risk of savers.

Savers, whether they invest directly or indirectly, are passive individuals who keep aside part of their income instead of spending it. They are passive because they give their money to others who are the ultimate users of money. These ultimate users of money are the true investors as they actually employ the savers' money in projects designed to earn more money. The project may produce goods or services. The savers do not produce goods and services, which is why they are passive. What the economy needs are the active investors who set up the projects to produce goods and services.

While being passive investors, we will still contribute to money earning more money by sharing our resources indirectly with the intermediaries who will use our money to lend further our money to those who have use of the money. Examples of indirect sharing are banks, corporate entities, insurance companies or voluntary associations who cater to the needs of a specific group of people, or microfinance companies.

In all indirect investments, your expectation is that you will get your money back as agreed by the intermediary; however, the risk is that the intermediary will fail to repay your invested amounts.

Banks guarantee the return of your invested amounts with the agreed return. But bank guarantees are as sound as the guaranteeing bank. The bank may fail. Similarly, insurance companies can fail to honor their guaranteed amounts. They can go bankrupt. The entity may fail, the bank or the insurance company or the company that issued shares to you may go bankrupt by the time you reclaim your money. Despite these risks, indirect sharing with the economy through the intermediaries is the only way to protect your money investments from the inflation. The challenge is to entrust your money to financially sound entities.

An economy with just savings that are not gainfully invested cannot assure "growth" in the production of goods and services. The savings not invested just go into a liquidity pool, and the result is that the prices of goods, services, and assets go up since there will be more money chasing the same stock. If more goods, more services, and more assets are available constantly, then more savings may not lead to higher prices. The society then will be richer because more of its members will own more of the assets or have access to more goods and services. This is the growth that the current economics seeks as ideal, based on its assumption that all of us like to continue to amass more wealth. Unfortunately, given our selfishness and greed, that assumption is correct. So, the world seeks acquisitive economic growth. But the world has limited potential to go on producing more goods, and the process impoverishes the earth, the environment that we all share, while it may enrich the individual members of the society. The growth economics seeks to enrich us at the expense of our own children, enrich the present generation at the expense of future generations.

If more goods cannot be produced with savings, we will see prices of goods rising. Those who own the goods and assets will get richer. Those who have yet to acquire the goods they need will need more money to buy them, so they will get poorer. More growth and wealth building thus has built-in inequality and poverty. Inequality arises from the inequality in the ability to earn and save money. Given the same freedom to all of us, some of us will always make more money than the rest of us. Those who earn more money will use their savings to buy more goods and assets and acquire more financial wealth. They will demand more goods and assets and drive up the prices further. As wealth accumulates in the hands of some people, it becomes more distant for others to acquire. Poverty comes through the rise in prices with more saved money demanding the same stock of goods or savers willing to pay higher prices for the coveted goods. Economic growth in terms of production of goods with limited resources will always bring more poverty through increasing prices and more inequality as a result where the rich will have greater ability to acquire the scarce goods.

Fortunately for all of us, an interesting solution to the potential poverty and inequality of physical economic growth has already emerged. Salvation lies in the production of services. Instead of earning our income from the material goods and spending our income to acquire goods, we can earn from providing services and spend by demanding services. Unlike goods, most of the services can have unlimited supply, as they use human skills, unlike the production of goods that uses limited natural resources. The so-called developed countries have already moved to a stage where over 70% of their citizens are employed in the services sector, only the rest in manufacturing and agriculture. We can get richer by acquiring more services, not more goods, without impoverishing the physical resources of the planet, by mutually supporting each other with the desired or required services rather than trying to sell one another more and more goods.

We can and do invest our services, skills, and non-monetary resources to earn returns not in terms of money alone, but in terms of access to a pool of services when in need. A cooperative society where all its members invest their personal resources and services is the answer of the economics of life, to the problem of sustainability of purely money-based economies seeking constant economic growth.

# The Book of Withdrawing Investments

Why Withdraw Savings?

How Much to Withdraw?

And if Investments or Savings Are Inadequate?

The Economics of Life at Our Assistance

To Save, Invest, and Withdraw Needs
Understanding of Money

Understanding Money

Understanding Wealth

The Illusion of Monetary Wealth

We cannot just keep our investments and marvel at them. We invest so we can use it someday to fund our expenses and to cover our spending. We need to withdraw money at the right time when we need to spend it in future.

When we need money to fulfil our current needs, and our earnings are not adequate, we have to withdraw the past savings and investments to make good the shortfall. After all, saving and investing were done in order to protect our future spending power.

When we need to use past savings and investments, we must withdraw all investments that we need.

Sometimes, our savings, which seemed large enough at the time we saved, prove to be inadequate to give us the required spending power because it now costs more to acquire the same set of goods and services we need. Sometimes the savings which were invested with the best advice at the time, prove to be inadequate because our investments' expected returns turn out to be lower than we had budgeted. Sometimes, the number or nature of our needs in the future turns out to be greater than we had anticipated at the time.

All these eventualities refer to our savings in money in the monetary economy. In all these cases, money was provided but fell short of future spending power. The investment advisors often say that if you invest more than you think you will need to withdraw, then invest more than the current price inflation dictates. But you must then have enough money to invest and must be willing to forgo your current consumption needs. Depriving you of resources to meet your current needs – is that good advice? Perhaps in the monetary economy, but what about our current lifestyles versus future needs?

It is here again that the economics of life come in to protect us. Of course, we need money to save and invest wisely, but we could have invested other resources than money to give us the future spending power, and without depriving us of our current consumption needs.

We can invest our time, effort, skills, and services now, with no immediate monetary return expected, but which acquire value in future when we need the alternative to spending power in money – by receiving from others their time or effort or skills and services. A service economy is more or less shielded from price inflation and is closer to a bargain economy, except that we "sell" our resources today to receive the same services in future.

# To Save, Invest, and Withdraw Needs Understanding of Money

Money is the key concept, the very basis and foundation of modern economies, which run with money. We save money, we invest money, and we use money. As investors in a monetary economy, we must understand the nature of money.

If you live in a barter economy, the money does not matter. But barter economies are hardly available now. All economic exchanges are driven by money. Hence, before we save and invest our money, we must understand the role of money. Money is our lifeblood in a money-based economy. Understanding the role and use of money will give us the ability to live, and live happily, in a money-based economy. So let us take a detour into understanding how money operates and drives the economy.

## The Value of Money as Our Withdrawing Power

Money is needed, valuable, and important only as a medium of purchase. Not only we the laypeople, but even the professional economists often forget this fact.

Money is a commodity. At our individual level, the more money we have, the bigger the saving and investing and income. Unfortunately, at the larger economy level, money is like any other commodity; the more there is of it, the less will be its value. This is the fundamental law of scientific economics – the price of any commodity is determined by its supply and demand for it. If the supply of money the commodity is more than the demand for it as a medium of exchange, if more people have more money, the value of money would decline. The relative purchasing power of money declines when more people have more money at their disposal. As a result, even at our individual level, more money at our disposal does not automatically translate into more saving or investing or income.

Money has three kinds of value – one, because it can purchase goods and services; two, because it can help earn more money; three, if it has purchasing power when we need it and withdraw. In other words,

1.  Money when spent has value only if it can help pay for our purchases now. Our spending power depends on the ability of money to purchase goods and services.
2.  Money when saved has value only if we can lend it to someone else who pays us for the use of money, or when we can invest it and earn more money out of the activity or the asset in which we invest. In other words, money must generate income when invested.
3.  Money has value only if it can help us pay for required purchases of goods and services, at the time we withdraw our investments. Money must retain its spending power over time as well as now; if price inflation takes place over time, the spending power of money will decline. The same amount of money now – say one hundred dollars – may not be sufficient to purchase the same amount of goods or services, due to inflation.

Money when stored under the mattress has no value in the present, unless spent or saved and invested. Stored money may have some value in the future only if, at that future time, it can either help pay for purchases or help earn more money.

Wealth means excess money, money that we earn in excess of our need to spend it, money that we save in excess of our future needs.

Wealth creation means earning more money than we need.

Wealth preservation means saving excess money and preserving the value of our investments in terms of purchasing power, so the monetary value of wealth does not decline.

Wealth management means investing the excess money to produce more money or to preserve the value of the savings.

The value of wealth depends upon the value of the assets in which we have invested our money. The same amount of wealth at the beginning may produce different returns for two individuals, depending upon what assets were acquired with the money. In other words, the value of your wealth depends upon the investment decisions you would have made in the past. Good wealth management means investment in earning assets that preserves or increases the value of your wealth.

Money that is saved, invested, or stored is considered wealth. In other words, wealth is defined as all the money that is not spent but is saved and invested.

In practice, our monetary wealth may turn out to be an illusion when we want to access and use our monetary wealth. How does this happen?

Wealth becomes illusory in two fundamental ways.

1. When we acquired wealth, we would have seen it as the ability to acquire our desired goods or assets in future. Yet the economic reality is that with inflation in prices of goods and assets, they become costlier than before. Effectively, the value of our wealth declines – what we hold now and can use to purchase goods or assets cannot buy the same quantity we could in future, so wealth becomes an illusion in terms of its utility and its purchasing power.

   Economists know this as price inflation. Inflation is the silent thief that steals away the value of our money by reducing its purchasing power, and our wealth. You could buy a Big Mac at one time for maybe 2 dollars, but it now costs 5 dollars- the same quantity as before. If you only saved two dollars, you would not be able to buy a full Big Mac now. The Economist Magazine in fact caught this day-to-day example and uses it to compare the relative value of money and inflation power in different countries, different economies. Even today, as we know, the same Big Mac sells for different prices in different countries. Past inflation or relative income levels may account for the anomaly. But that is the economic reality and defines the real value of wealth. What is true of a Big Mac burger is also true of other assets or consumption articles. The house we saved to acquire may have become costlier and beyond our budget. We may spend more of our income on food and have less money to invest or spend on pleasure; in some poorer countries, people end up spending nearly all their income on just food, while in relatively richer economies, people need to spend only 20/30 percentage of their income.

The value of money in terms of purchasing power comes down when more people have money and seek to buy the same stock of goods and services. We will bid up prices of the goods and services and we will pay more money for the same article or service; thus, our money will have less value and our monetary wealth too will have less value.

2.  Then there is another cause of decline in the value of our acquired wealth. When we want to use our acquired wealth, we may find that many others like us would have also acquired more wealth. When more of us have more money, money loses its value. All three kinds of value of money decline when there is more money around than before. That is why more monetary wealth may prove to be an illusion, in terms of the fundamental law of economics itself. As economists assume that all people are driven by greed for wealth and therefore for money, it assumes that the economic goal has to be a continuing acquisition of greater wealth, defined as greater and greater stock of money. Yet, money being a commodity, the more the monetary wealth with people, the less the value of their wealth, in terms of the science of economics itself.

While the demand/supply economic law is recognized and exists in reality, the professional economists ignore it. How?

At our individual level, many personal investment advisors take account of the inflation and its impact on our savings and our wealth. But this second way where our wealth loses value is not built into any scientific economic model – fact that our acquired wealth has a relative value, when compared to the wealth that other people acquire; in a successful prospering society, more and more people become wealthy; so more of us seek to buy goods and assets that become relatively costlier due to greater demand for them. When the stock of money in any economy keeps growing our relative personal wealth declines in value when compared to others – again lost value translates into an illusion. We may not have real wealth, only a nominal wealth. We save one hundred dollars now, but may have only 3 dollars in real value, 7 dollars turn out to be an illusion.

The professional economists' answer would be to build inflation and relative value of our wealth into our calculations of the required level of savings. Earn more and save more to keep up with declining value of wealth! And, add to further decline in the value of wealth! Keep pursuing the illusion of wealth!

How do we recognize and understand this illusory wealth? Take the investments we hold with our savings. The value of money saved and lent, in terms of its ability to generate further money, is measured by the interest rate that the lender can extract from the borrower. The more money available with more people, there are more lenders than borrowers, and the borrowers will pay less to the lenders for the use of money. Interest rates are the price of money saved; the price of saved money will come down when there is more of it. That is why, the greater the savings in a society, the lower the interest rate that the lenders (savers) can expect to get. So, the more people save, the less they earn on savings, as the value of their saved money declines. This is another manifestation of the illusion of wealth, even when money is saved. Most developed and some other countries have reached this stage, where savings have lost value; they do not earn any income. They are zero income economies, discouraging savings and favoring spending by us. Do not pursue wealth accumulation, just live from day to day.

*5.6*

# The Book of Sharing and Giving Away

Using Wealth – for Oneself

Leaving Wealth to Money Managers

Leaving Wealth for Your Children

Sharing Your Wealth

How Much to Share? When?

Sharing and Earning

Your Right to Share Your Wealth

The Sharing and Not Sharing Decision

The three ways of Wealth Sharing, Entrusting, or Giving Away

The real economics of life are all about using our wealth in the future – after all, that was the purpose for which we had saved and invested.

You must use your investments and wealth to satisfy your future needs – anticipated or accidental. As that future arrives, and as we must decide to use our accumulated wealth, let us remember the basic teaching of the economics of life that – what matters is life, not economics. Economics matter only to the extent that life does. Money matters to the extent that it helps make life better. Wealth matters but only to the extent that it enriches life. So, if our current income needs require the use of wealth for ourselves, we ought not to shy away from using wealth for ourselves.

If you have more wealth than you need to satisfy your needs, it may be of little "value", lost value of our wealth due to future price levels, inflation, and general distribution of wealth amongst us all, as we have noted earlier.

Instead of continued wealth accumulation and losing some of its value in future, we may consider another option - we use it to enrich the lives of others.

Unfortunately for all of us, most of us want to accumulate wealth for ourselves. Some of us want wealth for the future because we feel insecure about the future. Some of us want wealth because we want to feel superior to others around us. Some of us accumulate wealth because we earn much more money from our activities than we need. The result is that in any society, no matter how the wealth is measured, some people will always have more wealth than others. Those of us that have excess money, which is wealth, need to do something with that money. What do we do with excess wealth? Why not use it to improve the lives of others? And use wealth also for other purposes. What are the other options?

Some of us entrust our wealth to others to manage it for us. Leaving wealth in the hands of banks and money managers is intended to ensure that it will be used productively. But there is no guarantee that the money managers will necessarily use your wealth productively or be successful in doing it. They may not use your wealth in the same manner and direction that you would like to. You will find often that your wealth is not available to you in the future at the time you want it. Or that it has not produced the promised returns and accumulation is either less than expected or even negative.

Irrespective of the outcome of your investments managed by money managers, the wealth given to them is still your wealth; you have kept it for your own use later. To protect your wealth, you have to continue to manage the funds or assets given to financial intermediaries. What would be the purpose of managing your wealth portfolio given to intermediaries?

You need to take your wealth away from your chosen intermediaries if your wealth is eroding. But what if the intermediaries' performance is positive in using your wealth productively with satisfactory returns?

Most of us normal people usually think that the best and the only option open to us is to leave our wealth to our children. Leaving your wealth to money managers not for your own use, but for future use by your children, is justified by your need to ensure that they have a better future than otherwise. However, that is not the only option open to you, since our hard-earned and saved wealth in your children's hands may not necessarily be of the same value as it had for you, given the reduction in the value of money over time.

Besides, inheriting greater wealth will not necessarily increase the ability of your children to earn more money for themselves; as a more probable effect, they may relax in life with a significant inheritance and lose their independent initiative and ability to work and earn money for themselves. Or they may make unwise investments and squander your hard-earned wealth. Leaving your wealth to your children ends up giving more peace of mind and a sense of security to yourself than to your children.

You may also want to leave your wealth to your children, to give your children a head start over other people's children. This decision is a self-centric if not a selfish act. Even apart from the morality of the decision, it is not certain that your children will necessarily get the early start with your wealth that you desire. Many other people may also seek to and succeed like you in leaving their wealth to their children, in some cases perhaps even more than what you succeed in leaving to your children.

Given the reduction in the value of money as a result of more money being around, the value of your wealth in the hands of your children, in comparison with the wealth of others in the hands of their children, may be the same or less.

Inheritance of financial wealth does give an advantage to the inheritors, but only in comparison with and over those who do not inherit any wealth. However, if many people inherit much wealth, the society may seem to be rich, but the comparative value of money will negate the advantage of inherited wealth even in the next generation.

The only thing that happens with the passing of wealth from generation to generation is greater competition among those who inherit and greater inequality with those who do not inherit.

Since inheritance results in propagating inequality among future generations and creates and becomes a source of social conflict among different economic classes, that has led to some countries to impose an Inheritance Tax on the beneficiaries, to ensure that wealth is not used by the wealthy to the disadvantage of those who are not-so-wealthy and will not succeed in causing greater economic inequality in the society.

Actually, getting children started with more wealth than they need may even cripple them, stifle their enterprise, make them mere consumers of your wealth, not creators of wealth. The society needs wealth creators, not wealth spenders. You personally need wealth because you still estimate that you will have future needs to use the present wealth you have accumulated.

The economics of life dictates that your children live their own lives, independently of your wealth or dependence on it. Let your children earn, spend, save, invest, and create their own wealth. Let them not expect to get your wealth or guide their lives based on your wealth.

# Sharing Your Wealth

Other than just accumulating and passing your wealth on to your next generation, you can share your wealth with others who need money, monetary support, or other non-monetary support.

Sharing your wealth means you return to the society what you earned, saved, and invested, as a member of the society, not just spending it on oneself but on others in need. You, your children, and other members of the society all have a legitimate claim on your wealth. You have both the right and the responsibility to decide who you should share your wealth with. How, when and what you share with whom are decisions you can take and ought to take.

Let us review those options of sharing your wealth.

Sharing does not mean you ignore your own future needs or the future of your children; you need to provide as much as needed for your family needs. What is needed to be spent on maintaining the lifestyles of you and your own family throughout all stages of your life, you save and invest and use through your life.

It is the excess wealth after providing for your future needs that can be your pot for sharing with others.

That takes us to the economics of life that will dictate that you keep your excess wealth at the minimum level needed by your next generation, and the rest you reserve to share with the society or the community you are part of. You may share your wealth now during your lifetime or provide for your wealth to be used after your passing away – by writing a Will that lays down the rules to use your wealth after your passing away.

This last option will give you a sense of security while you are alive, by continuing to own and use your wealth while you are alive, and a sense of satisfaction that your wealth will be used for purposes dear to your heart even after your passing away. You can support your children and the segments of the society that need support, while giving a sense of security to your children that they will get support when they would be in need before or after your passing away.

You may thus divide your wealth into three parts – for use while you live, give to your children while you are alive and they need support, and the third part will be used to support the broader community of those who are in need. Timing to decide would be now, but its application (of the Will) may be later after your death.

Using wealth to enrich the lives of others is more satisfying and productive, more humane, and morally defensible than entrusting your wealth to banks and money managers, whether for your own future or for that of your children.

Sharing your wealth to enable other people to satisfy their needs is not just a moral imperative, not a giveaway. You earn something in return for sharing your resources, be it other contributions to your sharing pot or respect for you or even any direct help you may need from others.

If you have earned your money, saved, and invested and created wealth, you have the right to spend or share or even give away your wealth. Not even your children have necessarily any right to your genuinely earned wealth. Only you decide how much to share with others, just as you would decide how much to spend, save, invest, or withdraw.

How much to share with others is a difficult choice and decision. The reason is our human nature, our need for security, our normal choice to keep our wealth for ourselves and our family, and perhaps for several generations!

With whom do we share our wealth? A good reason not to share all your wealth with your own children is not to make your children dependent on you and discourage them from earning their own money. This is done by many billionaires like Bill Gates in the U.S. or Azim Premji in India.

Leaving your wealth for your children is justified if you ensure they will use your wealth not just for themselves but also to produce more jobs and more wealth for others, rather than just consuming more wealth than others.

Your using your own excess wealth to satisfy other people's needs and improve the lives of others has much more value for yourself and for the society.  By means of your own efforts, amass wealth if you succeed in earning more income than you need, but use your excess wealth to the benefit of the society during your own lifetime - that will ensure a better future for all the children of all human beings including yours - better than if you were to leave your wealth only to your own children. Mere accumulation of wealth may be a waste of your efforts and of the planet's resources. Spend your wealth for all. Spending your wealth for others is sharing it with them.

# The Three Ways of Wealth Sharing, Entrusting, or Giving Away

When you share your available resources or accumulated wealth with others in need, you are in effect giving away, if you share without any expectation of some return in the future.

If you are giving a loan of your time, resources, money, services, and establish your right to claim the same resources back, in a barter economy, or in the family, or even to a stranger, you are just sharing for now.

You can share your resources directly with the people in need. If shared without any expectation of reciprocation or return, you are giving away your resources. It is what we know as charity.

But you can also share your resources indirectly with the intermediaries who will use your money to lend further your money to those who have use of the money. Examples of indirect sharing are banks, corporate entities, insurance companies, or voluntary associations that cater to the needs of a specific group of people, or microfinance companies.

Entrusting your wealth to financial intermediaries where you retain the right to claim your funds back is an interim step until you decide to share it later. In the meantime, the financial intermediary uses your money to lend to others, and you are sharing your money indirectly for use in some productive part of the economy, but you are not giving away your resources for good.

When you buy the equity shares of corporate entities, you are sharing your resources with the share-issuing company, though the issuer of equity will not return your money directly, but you can find a buyer of your shares in the market.

When you buy insurance protection against certain risks, you pay a premium that insurance companies keep, and use the income to invest directly at their own risk. Return of your assured funds is conditional on a certain risk event happening such as disability or death.

In all indirect investments, your expectation is that you will get your money back as agreed by the intermediary; however, the risk is that the intermediary fails to repay your invested amounts or the return they promised. Banks, insurers, or corporate borrowers where we placed our wealth can fail or go bankrupt. Otherwise, you get your money back.

Another option for you is to entrust your money to mutual funds that invest in equity and debt securities for your account and at your risk. You can withdraw your funds by selling your Fund Shares back to the fund management company. But the amount invested or return on them are not guaranteed.

Despite these risks, indirect sharing with the economy through intermediaries is the only way to protect your money investments from the inflation that will otherwise erode the value of your savings. One way to contain the risk of loss is to entrust your money to financially sound entities. Few of us have the time or the knowledge required to manage our investments and protect our wealth by ourselves. Hence using intermediary money managers is a defensible placement of accumulated wealth. Yet, the objective of your personal economics must be for you to exercise your right to use this wealth at some point, during your lifetime or later.

If you do not wish to place your accumulated wealth with intermediaries, directly lending your resources is an option, whereby you share your wealth with your children or with others but with the right to withdraw your investments or expect a return.

It is the wealth that you use without any return expectation and without expecting the return of your invested sum, which means giving your wealth away. You have the right to decide to give away and a responsibility towards the larger society to share and give away your excess wealth as needed.

*Chapter Six*

# DEVELOPING A PERSONAL ECONOMIC PHILOSOPHY

KNOWING YOUR ECONOMICS OF LIFE FRAMEWORK

DEVISING YOUR OWN PERSONAL ECONOMICS –
THE KEY QUESTIONS

SUMMARIZING YOUR ECONOMICS OF LIFE MODEL –
TWO FRAMEWORKS

KNOWING YOUR PERSONAL ECONOMICS –
CURRENT STATUS AND CONSTRUCTING YOUR
FUTURE ECONOMIC PLAN

# Knowing Your Economics of Life Framework

Decision Making Framework for Economics of Life

Where do you belong?

Your Community's and Your Personal Rules

Rules of Your Economic Community

The economics of life are simple, and we have now completed our journey through the money governed economy to leave us free to decide what economics we would want or like to pursue, not the professional economists' economics, but our own personal economics.

Precisely because the economics of life is our own economics, and because we are all different by nature and by circumstances, the economics of life are unique to each of us. The economics of life is not a model that is prescribed by others, or by this book you have read and that works for all of us. That is why there are no Role Models to be followed and no universal rules of personal economics. We are what we are. Bill Gates is what he is. Even if we live in the U.S., we cannot just adopt the Bill Gates' personal economics, his economics of life. If we are a salaried executive or worker, Bill Gates model is not for us. If you live in a war-torn country, your economics will be radically different from a country at peace.

Yet, absence of straightforward Role Models does not constrain our making our own economic rules, our own economics of our own life, consistent with our own economic philosophy. The reason is that the economics of life is a framework for decision-making to build your own economics, based on your own life, your views – a framework that you use to build your own model if you like. The framework gives guidelines, not a fixed model with its rules, for us to determine our own economics.

The economics of life are also not unique to only some of us, say young ones. The framework will let you think about whatever your current age, or situation is, and let you build your own economics now, and always.

Let us summarize this decision-making framework you can use to determine your personal economics.

We live in communities – social, cultural, political, economic communities. Whether we like it or not, whether we are conscious of our belonging or not, we would always be part of different communities. Over time, as we become conscious of our place in the world, we may choose to shift from one community to another, though it is not always easy, and we may even choose to leave a community altogether, that is even more difficult. At least for most of us normal human beings.

Determine which community you are currently part of. As a student, you would be part of an academic community. Tomorrow, you may become part of a corporate community. But one thing is certain, unless you choose to retire to the Himalayas or adopt the vow of poverty as a Christian monk or priest, you will always be part of an economic community. And even after retirement, you would remain part of the economy.

When you are part of any community, you live by its rules and your own principles. Community rules are your constraints, your context. Your own principles are your philosophy, or part of it. The country and the town you live in will define their rules. Your employer or occupation will define its rules. Your family will define its rules. Even your religion will define its rules – the rules on the alms to others, or a complete vow of poverty if you choose to be a priest in any religion. This is your environment, your context.

By choosing your context and deciding how you deal with your context, you will define yourself.

Most of the time these personal principles are unknown to us because we are not conscious of them. We take them for granted. We live by them and do not seek to question or even clarify them. They are implicit in our behavior, our decisions, and our actions.

The first step in developing a personal economic philosophy is to consciously outline our own principles, our own philosophy. Then, to analyze them. And then to make a conscious choice – continue or change them. The choice is yours and mine. But the choice comes from awareness and free will. Yet our free will is not fully ours. We would have to live within the context and the rules set by the community we are part of. So, we need to assess the community rules and see whether our principles match, in which case we may continue our community affiliation, or they are in conflict, in which case we either need to reform our principles, or change the context, or even the community we belong to.

So, the first major exercise in developing a personal economic philosophy is to review your principles and the rules of the community you are or will be part of.

You can belong to many communities at a time, be a US citizen, with a particular religious community, and be young or old, and communities around causes – for example, Green Environment Advocacy group or investor community. But let us focus now on one community we will always belong to, wherever we are, that is the economic community. We must earn our living as they say. We have to accept that the economy will reward us for some activity, some contribution, that we have to perform or make. And the economy of which we are part will have its own rules.

One big rule and the context set by any economy is money; all economies are formed around money and use money as the medium of exchange for all our activities, and our contributions. We cannot just leave this monetary economy. We must accept and move along. After all our own success will also be mostly defined in terms of money. Unless you have already decided to retire to the Himalayas.

The second essential element of our personal economic philosophy will be the principles we set ourselves in relation to money – how we want to get it, what we want to do with it, and so on.

How do we think about money? First, we have a certain understanding of money – that needs to be examined. Then, we have our own attitudes towards money – those need to be made explicit. Then we must have our principles defined in terms of the decisions and actions we can take in the context of a money-driven economy.

Yet, the big lesson of this course in the economics of life is that we need not confine ourselves to the economies driven by money only. We can indeed examine other options where money will either be irrelevant or not have any significant relevance.

# Devising Your Own Personal Economics – The Key Questions

You can devise your own economics, designed to make you happy, by asking some overarching questions the answers to which will help you make your choices.

## Question 1

Do you want to remain a prisoner of money-driven economics and use and build personal economic plans uniquely in monetary terms?

## Question 2

Or do you want to use the economics of life and build your personal economics outside of the money-driven economy?

## Question 3

Can you completely leave the money-driven economy?

## Question 4

How to use the scientific economics model of using your scarce resources to generate the maximum benefit for you?

## Question 5

Or do you use the simple 6 step process of personal economics to work out your own economics of earning, spending, saving, investing, withdrawing, and sharing or giving away?

## Question 6

Or perhaps build your economics of life combining the pursuit of both monetary economics and your own personal economics?

Now you can also ask some specific questions about

## EARNING

### QUESTION 1

What do you want to earn, money and/or money equivalents, or non-monetary rewards? What do you value more than money – earning respect, or recognition, or some reward points you define?

### QUESTION 2

When do you want to earn and when to stop earning money and when do you want to replace money with some other rewards?

### QUESTION 3

How much to earn? When do you decide you have earned enough?

### QUESTION 4

For what purpose do you want to earn money or another reward?

### QUESTION 5

By what means do you want to earn? Working for others or for yourself? Work with money or without money? Work part-time combining employment and personal pursuit?

### QUESTION 6

What is sufficient for you – do you want to earn to be able to live comfortably now, or to provide for your future by investing and using it later? Or to pass on your accumulated wealth to your children, or share it with others or give away a part of it?

Now you can also ask some specific questions about

## SPENDING

### QUESTION 1

What do you want to spend, your money or your services and capabilities? Or both?

### QUESTION 2

How much money do you want to spend? And how do you decide the level of spending?

### QUESTION 3

Can you reduce your monetary spending needs? Your consumption?

### QUESTION 4

How do you decide how many of your personal resources do you want to spend? What are they?

Now you can also ask some specific questions about

SAVING

QUESTION 1

Does your income level permit you to save money?


QUESTION 2

If not, what do you wish to do? Change your work? Take help?


QUESTION 3

If your income level permits you to save, how much saving is enough?
How do you decide how much saving is enough for you?


QUESTION 4

Can you save your personal resources and capabilities?

Now you can also ask some specific questions about

## INVESTING

QUESTION 1

Have you invested your savings?


QUESTION 2

Have you taken professional investment advice?


QUESTION 3

Does your investment level assure you of accessibility when you need to withdraw? Does it give you enough return in the meantime?


QUESTION 4

What level of investment do you feel comfortable with?


QUESTION 5

If you have excess investments, would you withdraw some of them and either spend or share your money with others?


QUESTION 6

How do you invest your personal resources? Do you expect returns on investment of personal time, effort, services you invest in? Or do you wish to give your excess wealth away?

Now you can also ask some specific questions about

## WITHDRAWING INVESTMENTS

### QUESTION 1

Do you need to withdraw money? Is it imperative that you withdraw?

### QUESTION 2

For what purposes do you feel compelled to withdraw money?

To satisfy your own need for spending? Or do you withdraw to help your children?

Or you do not need to but want to withdraw to help others?

### QUESTION 3

Do you withdraw to share your wealth with others, with no returns expected?

### QUESTION 4

When do you withdraw money? Regularly or only for immediate needs, or have you reached the stage where you want to share your wealth?

### QUESTION 5

Do you feel fearful of withdrawing money? Unsure of future needs?

Or do you need to withdraw but prefer waiting until later to preserve your investments, using your money and wealth?

# Summarizing Your Economics of Life Model – Two Frameworks

Two Final Questions

You can build your economics of life based on your response to two final questions –

1. What is your age?
2. What is your starting point in modeling?

You can determine your personal economics framework as a model that gives you happiness that you seek.

The Economics of Life model using both money-driven and non-monetary economics is your own, unique, and simple model to follow.

Here are two frameworks, for young and old, to design your personal economics, using personal economics framework around money.

## IF YOU ARE YOUNG AND INCLINED TOWARDS PRONOUNCED TENDENCIES

| Your stage in life | Your Inclinations | | |
|---|---|---|---|
| **START YOUNG** | Normal | Prodigal | Philanthropic |
| | | | |
| Earn | **YES** | **YES** | **YES** |
| Spend | **YES** | **YES** | **YES** |
| Save | **YES** | **NO** | **YES** |
| Invest | **YES** | **NO** | **YES** |
| Withdraw investments | **YES** | **NO** | **YES** |
| Share or giveaway | **YES** | **NO** | **YES** |

If you are young, normal, or philanthropic, you ought to follow all six activities of a personal economic framework.

If you tend towards being prodigal, you will not be saving or investing money; so, you will have to find some non-monetary resources you need to earn, spend, save, and invest, and if possible, share your wealth.

# IF YOU ARE IN AN ADVANCED AGE AND INCLINED TOWARDS PRONOUNCED TENDENCIES

| Your stage in life | Your Inclinations | | |
|---|---|---|---|
| **START LATER IN LIFE** | Happy | Needy | Philanthrope |
| | | | |
| Earn | **NO** | **YES** | **YES** |
| Spend | **YES** | **YES** | **YES** |
| Save | **NO** | **NO** | **YES** |
| Invest | **NO** | **NO** | **YES** |
| Withdraw investments | **YES** | **NO** | **YES** |
| Share or giveaway | **YES** | **NO** | **YES** |

If you are retired and happy with your past savings, you can spend or perhaps even share your wealth. You do not need to earn and save and invest. You do not need to call upon your non-monetary resources. If you have non-monetary resources at your command, you can use them, too.

However, if you are retired and still need money, you need to earn and spend. You cannot save or invest or giveaway.

If you still want to be a philanthrope, you need to pursue all six activities of personal economics. And you further need to raise non-monetary resources and live a philanthropic life.

# KNOWING YOUR PERSONAL ECONOMICS – CURRENT STATUS AND CONSTRUCTING YOUR FUTURE ECONOMIC PLAN

While reviewing the two possible frameworks dictated by your age and inclinations towards money, you can also construct your own model, following the community you are part of – neighborhood, religious congregation, fellow students and any other.

To help you construct your own model of economics, use the template that follows – it is blank, so fill it up with your real-life state; this is not your goal but your current status, to understand your economic plight.

| Your stage in life | Your Current State | | |
|---|---|---|---|
| | | | |
| Earning? | | | |
| Spending? | | | |
| Saving? | | | |
| Investing? | | | |
| Withdrawing investments? | | | |
| Sharing or giving away? | | | |

The above template describes where you are in life, at what stage in the Economics of Life.

NOW YOU CAN DESCRIBE YOUR DESIRED GOAL, USING THE
SAME TEMPLATE TO DECIDE WHERE YOU WANT TO GO –

USE THE BLANK TEMPLATE TO DESCRIBE YOUR GOAL.

| Your stage in life | Your Economic Goal | | |
|---|---|---|---|
|  |  |  |  |
| Earning? |  |  |  |
| Spending? |  |  |  |
| Saving? |  |  |  |
| Investing? |  |  |  |
| Withdrawing investments? |  |  |  |
| Sharing or giving away? |  |  |  |

Let this be your Personal Economic Plan – for Money.

NOW USE THE TEMPLATE TO CONSTRUCT YOUR PERSONAL ECONOMICS OF LIFE FOR EACH OF THE RESOURCE AT YOUR DISPOSAL – WITH EACH NON-MONETARY RESOURCE – **KNOWLEDGE, SKILL, TIME, SERVICE**

| Your stage in life | Your Resource | | |
|---|---|---|---|
|  |  |  |  |
| Earning? |  |  |  |
| Spending? |  |  |  |
| Saving? |  |  |  |
| Investing? |  |  |  |
| Withdrawing investments? |  |  |  |
| Sharing or giving away? |  |  |  |

The first two frameworks show you what personal economic model will be right for you, as against the general economic model.

The subsequent framework lets you describe your personal economic status, and as against that – your personal economic goal – that will be measured in money.

The final framework can be a blank slate to fill-out with your own non-monetary resources and develop a plan for each resource.

# Chapter Seven

# EPILOGUE AND AN INVITATION TO RE-JOIN

Here is The Final Word on your economics of life.

Whatever your model, described above, pursue happiness in life, with money or other resources, mind your own economics, do not heed the economists' public policies except where they concern and impact your model of economics of your own life –

Be economically happy.

# AN INVITATION TO SHARE YOUR VIEWS

This is the epilogue of the book, our coming together as reader and author. But it is not the final word or epilogue to our relationship.

Let us come together again by knowing "your own" personal economics – thoughts, models, frameworks, or simply your reactions to what the book has covered.

You may use any of the following options to share your views:

- Email : book@dcanjaria.com

- Website : www.dcanjaria.com

- Facebook – X/Twitter – Medium – GoodReads

Let us remain in touch.

# ABOUT THE AUTHOR

D. C. Anjaria has been a student of economics at the undergraduate level studying Commerce, at the post graduate level studying Business Administration, and then working as an international banker and financial markets professional.

At each stage, he has seen the value of economics as a social science, and its limitations at the personal level. His work with a leading American bank – Citibank, brought him in contact with diverse geographic and cultural milieus, in India, Mauritius, West Africa, Middle East, and Europe. He has seen people with diverse attitudes towards money, and people with both successful management of their economic lives and those who suffered from lack of understanding of money and economics.

In the end, the author managed to understand and shape his own economic life using his global exposure. He has also understood how the professional economists and governments develop their economic policies, while advising governments in India and Indonesia in public policy and regulatory structures for money-driven economies.

Using this lifelong experience, he has developed an understanding of personal economics as opposed to practice of economics at the macro-economy level. He now has crystallized and shared his "economic wisdom" for the benefit of the non-economist human beings, through this book as the distillation of the economic wisdom.

The author is one of you – a non-economist who has presented his economic wisdom with you and invites you to share your economic wisdom with him – D. C. Anjaria.